Gothic Knits

Gothic Knits

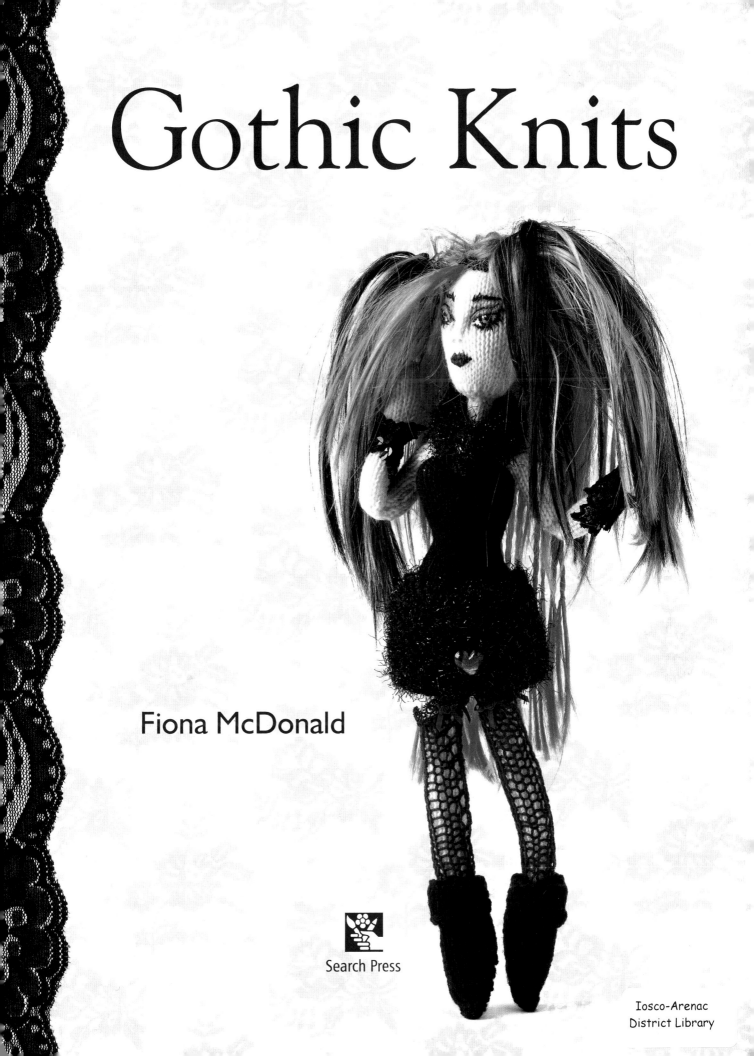

Fiona McDonald

Search Press

First published in Great Britain 2012

Search Press Limited
Wellwood, North Farm Road,
Tunbridge Wells, Kent TN2 3DR

Text copyright © Fiona McDonald 2012

Photographs by Roddy Paine at Roddy Paine
Photographic Studio, and Paul Bricknell at Search Press
Photographic Studio

Photographs and design copyright © Search Press Ltd.
2012

ISBN: 978-1-84448-648-9

The Publishers and author can accept no responsibility
for any consequences arising from the information,
advice or instructions given in this publication.

Suppliers
If you have difficulty in obtaining any of the materials
and equipment mentioned in this book, then please visit
the Search Press website for details of suppliers:
www.searchpress.com

Printed in Malaysia

Dedication

To my brothers, Ken, Bill and Ian

Acknowledgements

My first thanks go, as always, to Isabel
Atherton of Creative Authors, agent
extraordinaire. Also a huge thank you
to the Search Press team for making my
dreams come true, especially Roz Dace and
Katie Sparkes. Thank you!

Contents

The Goths

Introduction

Night is falling and the wind is in the trees, dogs howl at the moon and cats are about, eyes gleaming in the dark. Look out! What's that behind you? Only a shadow. A twig cracks and your breath freezes, flesh creeps and a scream begins to work its way up your throat. Someone steps in front of you, blocking your way. Tall, dark and handsome or beautiful beyond belief, the stranger in your path, though weirdly seductive, makes you gasp with fear.

But who (or what) is the creature in this story? We all recognise him, her or it from the ghost stories of our childhood, the late-night horror movies we watched and then were too scared to go to bed, and of course the darkest creations of our imaginations that become all too real as our head hits the pillow and the light is switched off.

Now the the stuff of nightmares has been knitted and stuffed – the vampires and villains, maidens and monsters, have been immortalised in yarn, fashioned into dolls using those fearful implements, the knitting needles, and brought to life by their cunning creator – Fiona McDonald.

There are nine petrifying patterns to choose from, in two different sizes – the small but sinister Amorosa, Gwendolyn, Mercy, Sebastian and D'Anton, each measuring around 50cm (20in) tall and, standing at 60cm (23in) tall, the hugely hideous Julian, Patience, Beatrice and Violetta. Don't feel obliged to simply reproduce exactly what the author of this book has prescribed – take inspiration from her designs and create characters based on your own ghastly imaginings. But be warned – parts of some of these creatures are small and detachable, so they are not suitable playthings for very young children. And for those of a nervous disposition – you'd better sleep with the light on, just in case.

Before you begin ...

The dolls in this book are specifically designed for adults and older children. However, younger children will love the dolls too, but if you intend to give one to a child who is under three years old, then the following safety precautions should be taken:

- The doll must not have any small, detachable parts that may get chewed off and choked on.
- The felt eyes and lips must be stitched on as well as, or instead of, gluing. Otherwise embroider the features straight on to the knitted face.
- Do not use buttons, press studs, hooks and eyes, or anything else that could possibly be a choking hazard.

Materials

Each pattern includes a list of the yarns, needles and other materials and equipment needed for that particular project. Please note that all the quantities of yarn given in this book are to be regarded as approximate, and the colours and types of yarns, trimmings and embellishments you use depend on both availability and personal preference.

Yarns

Patons yarns kindly supplied the yarn for the dolls in this book. I used Cleckheaton Country 8-ply (DK/double knitting) wool for the dolls' bodies because I found it a lovely wool to work with and it has a great range of skin tones. While I would recommend using this yarn for making the dolls, any 8-ply yarn (also known as double knitting or light worsted) will give equally good results. Whichever yarn you choose, it is a good idea to use the same brand throughout your knitting as not all yarns are the same. I prefer to use pure wool, but there is no reason why an acrylic or acrylic mix could not be used, as long as it is a smooth and not a textured yarn.

For the hair, use whatever takes your fancy: straight wool, bouclé, fancy yarn, fluffy yarn or nylon doll hair, for example. Knitted and unravelled wool makes lovely wavy hair. It can be thick, thin, short or long, red, green, brown or any other colour. Try adding ribbon, silk embroidery thread or chunky yarn that looks like dreadlocks.

For the clothing I have used Cleckheaton Country 8-ply (double knitting) yarn as well as 5-ply (sport), 4-ply (fingering) and some cheap, novelty yarns that I had in my huge hoard at home. I suggest you experiment with what you have available, and you may well come up with something even better than the original.

ABBREVIATIONS

I have tried to keep the patterns as simple as possible, and the only abbreviations you need to remember are:

K knit

P purl

st(s) stitch(es)

K2tog knit two stitches together

P2tog purl two stitches together

GS garter stitch (consecutive rows of knit stitch only)

SS stocking stitch (alternating rows of knit and purl)

inc increase (I always increase by knitting into the front then the back of the stitch before slipping it off the left-hand needle)

dec decrease (by knitting two stitches together unless specified otherwise)

rep repeat

beg beginning

rem remaining

Knitting needles and crochet hooks

You will need three sizes of needle – 3mm (UK 11, US 3), 4mm (UK 8, US 6) and 7mm (UK 2, US 11) – and a 3mm (UK 3/0, US 0 or D) crochet hook. The basic dolls are knitted using 3mm (UK 11, US 3) knitting needles, which is smaller than you would normally use with double knitting. This is because the knitted body of the dolls needs to be tighter than a knitted garment would be. If the tension is too loose, then the stuffing will be visible and the doll will be unshapely. If you find it too difficult to knit with the double-knitting yarn on 3mm (UK 11, US 3) needles, then experiment with slightly larger needles until you find a comfortable size.

I use a 3mm (UK 3/0, US 0 or D) crochet hook for picking up stitches and transferring them to a knitting needle, and also for hooking hair through knitted scalps. You may prefer to use a slightly larger hook when using thicker yarn.

Other items you will need

Polyester fibrefill: I use the type of stuffing found in cheap pillows, or carded fleece, to stuff the dolls with. Polyester fibrefill is probably the easier to obtain, and is the better of the two for stuffing the heads. Carded fleece gives a lovely weight to the dolls but is heavier and harder to needlesculpt. In the end it comes down to availability and personal preference.

TENSION

The yarns used in this book all give a similar tension range (gauge), which is 22 stitches to 10cm (4in) when used with 4mm (UK 8, US 6) needles and stocking stitch. Any yarn that states this tension on the ball band is therefore suitable for use with the patterns in this book.

Stuffing tool: I use an old, cheap, bristle paintbrush for stuffing the dolls. The bristles help hold the stuffing as you push it down, for example, a long leg.

Tapestry needle: used for sewing up seams and needlesculpting the face and body where necessary. I use an ordinary sized one, but you can use a doll-making needle if it is easier.

Glue: I use clear, fast-drying craft glue. You could use white craft or wood glue, but they take much longer to dry.

Felt: white felt is used for making the eyes; red or pink felt for lips.

Chopsticks and/or plastic straws: these are used to give your doll a strong, rigid back.

Sticky tape: wrapped around the 'backbone' to help to hold it in place within the doll's body.

Thin card: for making templates for the eyes and lips.

Paints, marker pens and pencils: to add colour to the faces, adding depth and a sense of drama, you will need acrylic or water-based paints in white, black, pinks, reds, purples and browns, together with a very fine paintbrush. For greater control, use fine-tipped, water-based marker pens instead. These may also be used as an alternative to stitching for colouring the eyes and lips, though a more striking effect can generally be achieved with stitching. A pencil and/or a vanishing marker pen is useful for marking on the positions of your doll's features before gluing or stitching them on, and for drawing the details on to the eyes and lips before attaching them to the doll's face.

Nylon hair extensions and dolls' hair: I have used these for the hair on some of the dolls. You will also need small elastic hairbands for securing the hair in bunches.

Hooks and eyes and press studs: these are used for fastening the dolls' clothes around the waist or neck, but avoid using them if you intend to give your doll to a young child to play with.

Sewing needles: these are used for sewing on press studs and other fastenings, hair, eyebrows, embellishments, etc. and for embroidering the eyes and lips.

Scissors: you will need a pair of sharp scissors for trimming threads and for cutting out felt shapes for the eyes and lips.

Pins: these are useful for positioning the doll's eyes, lips, ears, etc. before stitching them in place, and for holding seams together before stitching the clothes.

Threads: you will need six-stranded embroidery thread – silk is best, though polyester or cotton can also be used – to embroider on the eyes, eyebrows and lips. The main colours you will need are blue, black, brown, purple and red. You will also need ordinary sewing thread for general sewing, such as stitching on embellishments and pieces of lace.

Embellishments: add finishing touches to your doll in the form of lace, fabric flowers, ribbon, fancy buttons and beads. These can be sourced from fashion stores and craft stores, or rescued from old items of clothing and jewellery. Once you start looking, you will be amazed how many you will find – and they are perfect for making a doll uniquely yours!

TIP

When stuffing your doll, use smallish pieces so that you don't get big, misshapen lumps where you don't want them. Legs are quite difficult to stuff evenly and smoothly – massage the stuffing into place, and avoid over-stuffing. As a general rule, try not to put so much stuffing in that the knitting stretches apart.

Hair

The hair is your doll's crowning glory, and it plays a major part in defining your doll's character. Make it as eye-catching as you want by using long lengths of fancy yarn in striking colours and textures, or use brightly coloured hair cut from fake hairpieces, fancy-dress wigs and dolls' hair. I like my dolls to have hair that looks as though it is growing out of their heads. There are three ways of doing this:

Stitched-on hair

Bundles of hair are stitched on to the scalp, following the instructions provided.

The rooted method

For this you will need a crochet hook. A 3mm (UK 3/0, US 0 or D) crochet hook is just about right, depending on the thickness of the yarn. For very thick yarn, a larger crochet hook might be better. You can use any kind of yarn you think will make beautiful hair.

1. Find a book or a piece of stiff board that is the height of the length of hair you want. Wrap the yarn around the book or board, not too tightly. Before it gets too bulky, cut through the wound yarn at one end of the book only; the doubled lengths of yarn each form two strands of hair.

2. Begin by working round the hairline, starting above the middle of the forehead. Insert the crochet hook under a knitted stitch. Hook the loop of the folded hair strand and pull it through the stitch. Now pass the ends of the hair strand through the loop and pull it tight to knot it around the knitted stitch. Continue around the head and then fill in the rest of the scalp.

3. When the hair is done, trim to the desired length or style.

Using fake hair

For some dolls I use cheap, synthetic hair extensions, hair scrunchies and fancy-dress wigs to create amazing hair colours and textures.

1. Carefully disassemble the hair accessory so that you are left with a strip of fake hair sewn along the top, and wind this around the scalp of the doll. Start at the centre of the doll's head and work outwards in a spiral. If you are using hair from a wig, cut a section from the wig that fits comfortably on your doll's head and pin it in place.

2. Stitch the hair in position using a thread that matches the scalp colour of the doll.

3. Cut shorter lengths of hair for a fringe or to fill odd spaces.

Assembling the bodies

All of the dolls' bodies are put together in the same way. The order in which you assemble your doll is entirely up to you. You may prefer to make the head first, shape it and sew on the eyes and lips before attaching it to the rest of the body; alternatively, you might prefer to sew all the body parts together and then form and stitch the face last. Whichever way you do it, use the instructions given here for general guidance, but remember that your doll is your creation, and you can give him, her or it any character you want.

Torso

To make the neck stiff you will need something firm to put in it. You could use chopsticks or two or three plastic straws taped together. These dolls are not designed for very young children to play with, but if you do knit them for a child use plastic straws rather than chopsticks.

1. Take the body and fold it in half lengthwise, with right sides together.

2. Backstitch up the seam from the base to the top of the neck. Neaten off the thread and turn right side out.

3. Wrap sticky tape around the chopsticks or straws. The final layer should have the sticky side facing outwards.

4. Wrap some polyester fibrefill around the stick and insert it into the body and up into the neck. Make sure the stick doesn't protrude out through the base of the body and extends a little beyond the top of the neck.

5. Stuff the body firmly with polyester fibrefill around the backbone chopstick or straws. Stitch the base closed.

Legs

1. Fold each leg in half lengthwise, with right sides facing. For most of the legs, back stitch down from the top, stopping where it begins to narrow. Backstitch up from the toe until it narrows at the ankle.

2. Turn right side out and finish stitching the narrow areas from the outside with mattress stitch.

3. With tiny bits of polyester fibrefill begin to stuff each foot, ankle and leg. Make the legs as even as possible.

4. When each leg is stuffed, pin them in position under the torso and stitch in place. There are two ways of doing this. Either flatten the top of the leg and whip stitch it to the base of the torso, or pin around the top of the leg, giving the leg a more rounded form, then mattress stitch the leg to the torso. The flattened version works well for seated dolls whereas the rounded version is better if your doll is going to be standing.

5. To form the feet, bend the leg 3–4cm (about 1½in) from the toe end (you can make the feet larger or smaller). Using the same coloured yarn as the leg, use mattress stitch to hold the bend in place around the back of the foot.

Beatrice's legs and feet.

Arms

For the larger dolls, sew up the arms and stuff them in the same way as the legs, only the arms will need to be stitched together with the wrong sides facing, unless you are very good at turning narrow knitted tubes. Shape the tops of the arms and fit them snugly to the shoulders, pin them in place and mattress stitch around each arm to attach them to the torso. Make sure the thumbs are pointing inwards!

The smaller dolls have shaped arms that need to be made up in two parts. Begin by stitching from the tips of the fingers up to approximately 1cm (½in) below the elbow, then from the top of the arm to about 1cm (½in) above the elbow. Turn right side out (unless you have stitched with the wrong sides facing). Stuff the hand and lower arm, then stitch the elbow shut and stuff the upper arm. Attach the arms as described above.

Beatrice's upper body, showing the legs joined to the body, and the arms (compare them with the arms of the smaller dolls shown below, which are shaped).

Adding form to the torso

If you have a long doll-making needle this will be easier to use, but sculpting the torso can be done with an ordinary tapestry needle. You will need a long length of the same yarn that you used for the torso.

Female torsos

Gothic girls have shapely figures that are easy to needlesculpt following the steps below.

1. To form the buttocks and belly button, insert the needle in through the back, leaving a long tail thread. Bring the needle out in the area of the belly button and pull firmly on the thread. Make a small stitch and push the needle back into the torso. Bring the needle and thread out between the legs and pull firmly. Take the thread up to a point on the doll's back that is a fraction lower than the belly button and pass the needle through into the torso at that point. Bring it back out between the legs again. Pull the thread firmly, and the yarn on the outside of the torso will pull the buttocks into shape. Make a small securing stitch and neaten all the threads.

2. For the breasts, take another length of torso-coloured yarn and thread it into a doll-making needle or a tapestry needle. Push the needle into the torso from the back and bring the needle out at the side of one breast, at the top. Push the needle back through and make a small stitch, then pass the thread across to come out on the other side of the breast. Pull the yarn very gently. Work backwards and forwards from one side of the breast to the other, gradually working your way downwards and following the shape of the breast. Do the same on the other side of the torso for the other breast.

3. To make a small, neat waist, run a thread of body colour in and out of the stitches from centre back to centre front, in both directions. Make the stitches small and even. Pull the waist thread firmly but not too tight. Tie the ends together and neaten by passing the ends back into the body.

Male torsos

Boy Goths are strong and handsome, and need a physique to match. Their buttocks and belly button are formed in exactly the same way as those of the female Goths, but the similarity ends there. Instead of a waist and breasts, the male torso is given an impressive set of abdominal muscles and a firm chest.

To create a nicely sculpted abdomen, some of the stitching will lie on the surface of the knitting and some will be inside the torso, using the tension of the front and back surfaces to aid the sculpted form. Generally, you should aim to form a line down the front of the torso, from the middle of the chest to just above the belly button. You may prefer to create two separate lines, a short one to define the chest, a small gap and then a longer one for the stomach muscles.

You can also shape the spine by making a line of stitches down the back, anchored at some point on the front, such as the belly button.

1. Make the vertical stitch first by threading a needle with a long length of yarn and inserting the needle from the back between the shoulder blades (if he had any). Bring the needle out through the top of chest, but well below the neck.

2. Either insert the needle back into the torso a short way down to create a separate chest or take the thread all the way down to just above the belly button and insert the needle there. Take the needle straight through the torso and bring it out through the back. Pull the thread firmly and make a tiny securing stitch.

3. If you are shaping the chest and abdomen separately, now bring the needle back through to the front of the torso just below the chest and pass the thread back through at a point just above the belly button. Take the needle straight through the torso and bring it out through the back. Pull the thread firmly and make a tiny securing stitch, as in step 2.

4. You now need to make two or three parallel lines across the centre vertical line. Begin by taking the needle back through the torso (to the front but to one side of the centre line) at a point above the abdomen, at the base of the chest.

5. Take the thread across horizontally and push the needle into the centre line and straight out through the back. Push the needle back through to the same position on the front of the torso and make a similar horizontal stitch on the opposite side.

6. Repeat steps 4 and 5 for the abdominal muscles further down the torso. Pull the thread firmly but gently after each stitch, and neaten the thread when you have finished.

On left-hand page: full view of Beatrice showing needlesculpting; from left to right at bottom of page: front view, side view and back view. From top to bottom on this page: full body, front view and back view of D'Anton.

Head

1. Take the head and fold it in half lengthwise, right sides together.

2. Backstitch from the top of the head to the base, leaving a wide neck opening.

3. Stuff the head firmly but don't overstuff (if the stitches stretch so that the stuffing shows through the stitching, you have probably overstuffed it).

4. Push the head down on to the backbone and the top of the neck. The neck should go up into the head for a couple of centimetres or so. Leave some neck showing as long necks are elegant, but do not perch the head at the very top of the neck either. Mattress stitch the head to the neck. If the neck opening is too large then gather up a little of the base of the head at the back until it fits.

Forming the face

When forming the face, refer to the photograph of your chosen doll to achieve the exact shape of the nose, eyes and cheeks; or use your imagination and devise your own 'look' for your doll, perhaps sketching it out on paper beforehand.

Nose

1. Take a tapestry needle and thread it with the same coloured yarn as the head. Leaving a long tail thread, push the needle into the head somewhere not too noticeable (such as the back of the neck or head) and bring it out on one side of the nose. Take the needle back through close to where it came out to make a tiny stitch, and bring it out on the other side of the nose. Pull the thread gently to tighten it across the back of the nose, then repeat a couple of times until the nose is the required shape.

2. To define the nostrils, push the needle under the nose and bringing it out where one of the nostrils would be. Pull gently on the thread and take the needle back through, bring it out on the other side of the nose. Repeat for the other nostril. Push the needle back through the head and neaten off the thread.

Eye sockets

To shape the eye area, take another thread and thread it through a tapestry needle. Push the needle into the head from the back and bring it out to one side of the nose, where the inner corner of one eye would be. Make a small stitch and push the needle back through the head. Pull the thread gently so that the eye socket begins to form. Bring the thread back through at the inner corner of the other eye and repeat. Form the outer corners of the eyes in the same way, securing and neatening off the thread when you've finished.

Make sure the eyes are the same size and, unless you intend your doll to have odd eyes, symmetrical. You might find it helpful to dot in the corners of each eye before needlesculpting using a pencil or vanishing fabric marker.

Top of Beatrice's neck, showing join to head.

Side view of Beatrice's head. Notice that Beatrice has a flatter, broader nose than some of the other dolls. This is achieved by pulling the thread more gently, creating a looser stitch than you would for a narrower nose. For a short, button nose, use fewer stitches than you would for a longer nose.

Cheekbones

The male Goths have very pronounced cheekbones. This is achieved by bringing the thread through from the back of the head to just under where the cheekbone would be. Make a tiny stitch and push the needle through to the other side of the face, just below where the other cheekbone would be, and pull the thread firmly. Continue working back and forth in this way, making a line of three or four stitches underneath each cheekbone. When you are happy with the result, push the needle back through the head, secure and neaten off the thread.

Eyes

It can be difficult to embroider in detail on to knitting, so use a piece of white felt cut into the shape of the eye to embroider on to, and use two or three strands of six-stranded embroidery thread to stitch with. As you stitch, make sure you catch in some of the knitting underneath to secure the eyes firmly to the face. When drawing on the eye detail and positioning the eyes, refer closely to the photograph of your chosen doll, or use your imagination to dream up some horrid creations of your own. And in true Goth style, don't be afraid to overdo the eye make-up.

1. Trace two of your chosen eyes from the templates and transfer them on to card, then draw around these on to white felt. Your two eyes need to be mirror images of each other.

2. Cut out the felt eyes then draw on the eye detail (the irises, pupils and upper eyelids) in pencil or using fine-tipped coloured marker pens.

3. Pin the felt eyes in position on the face and embroider on the detail following the notes given with the doll you are making. For the irises, you might prefer to use coloured marker pens instead of stitching.

4. To give the eye depth and drama, use a fine-tipped water-based marker pen or very thin washes of acrylic or watercolour paint to tint the eye socket. Be careful if using paint that the colour doesn't bleed into the white of the eye; if you do use paint you might prefer to tint the eye socket and let it dry before attaching the eye.

5. Mark in the eyebrows lightly with a pencil or vanishing fabric marker, then embroider them on.

Mouth

Choose your mouth from the templates provided, then transfer it on to card and cut out the mouth from red felt. Stitch the mouth on to the doll, following the notes given with the instructions for the doll.

Ears

Take each ear and use the excess yarn to gather the longer sides of the ear slightly. Pin in position on the side of the head and stitch in place.

PATIENCE

Now Frankenstein's monster has a female companion, though instead of being created in the laboratory by a mad scientist, this slightly softer version has been knitted. Her striking scar, odd legs and weirdly misaligned eyes are a clue to her strange beginnings. Tall and long-legged, with pale skin, blood-red lips and white hair, this ethereal beauty will make any monster's heart miss a beat.

What you need

Note that these are the specific things you need in order to make Patience; all the general items required are listed on pages 9–10.

Needles

Knitting needles in sizes 3mm (UK 11, US 3), 4mm (UK 8, US 6) and 7mm (UK 2, US 11)

Yarn

8-ply (DK) yarn in off-white for the head, torso and arms
8-ply (DK) yarn in black and red for the legs and boots
4-ply (fingering) yarn in black for the fingerless gloves
5-ply (sport) yarn in dark purple for the dress
5-ply (sport) yarn in light purple for the pants

Embroidery threads

Purple, black, red, white and variegated red (for the lips)

Paints

Acrylic paints, watercolour paints or fine-tipped water-based marker pens in purple and brown

Embellishments and extras

Large, black fabric rose
Press studs for the top of the dress
Variegated eyelash yarn in pale pastel shades for the hair

NOTES

See the general notes on pages 12–13 for knitting and stuffing the dolls, and follow the instructions on pages 14–17 for sewing the body parts together and needlesculpting the torso and face.

BODY PARTS

Head

Make one.

Using 8-ply (DK) yarn in off-white and 3mm (UK 11, US 3) needles, cast on 3 sts.

Row 1: inc in each st [6 sts].

Row 2: purl.

Row 3: inc in each st [12 sts].

Row 4: purl.

Row 5: inc in each st [24 sts].

Row 6: purl.

Row 7: inc 1 st at each end of row [26 sts].

Row 8: purl.

Row 9: inc 1 st at each end of row [28 sts].

Row 10: purl.

Row 11: inc 1 st at each end of row [30 sts].

Row 12: purl.

Row 13: inc 1 st at each end of row [32 sts].

Row 14: purl.

Row 15: inc 1 st at each end of row [34 sts].

Row 16: purl.

Row 17: cast on 5 sts, knit to end of row [39 sts].

Row 18: cast on 5 sts, purl to end of row [44 sts].

To shape the nose:

Row 19: K21, inc in next 2 sts, K21 [46 sts].

Rows 20–22: SS for 3 rows.

Row 23: K21, K2tog twice, K21 [44 sts].

Row 24: purl.

Row 25: inc 1 st at each end of row [46 sts].

Rows 26–31: SS for 6 rows.

Row 32: P2tog at each end of row [44 sts].

Row 33: K2tog at each end of row [42 sts].

Row 34: P2tog at each end of row [40 sts].

Row 35: K2tog at each end of row [38 sts].

Row 36: purl.

Row 37: K2tog along row [19 sts].

Row 38: purl.

Row 39: K2tog four times, K3, K2tog four times [11 sts].

Row 40: P2tog at each end of row [9 sts].

Row 41: K and cast off as you go.

Ears

Make two.

Using 8-ply (DK) yarn in off-white and 3mm (UK 11, US 3) needles, cast on 4 sts.

Row 1: inc in each st [8 sts].

Row 2: purl.

Row 3: inc in each st [16 sts].

Row 4: purl.

Row 5: K2tog at each end of row [14 sts].

Row 6: P2tog at each end of row [12 sts].

Row 7: K2tog along row [6 sts].

Row 8: purl and cast off as you go.

Torso

Make one.

Using 8-ply (DK) yarn in off-white and 3mm (UK 11, US 3) needles, cast on 46 sts.

Rows 1–14: SS for 14 rows.

Row 15: *K1, K2tog*, rep from * to * to end of row, ending with a K1 [31 sts].

To shape the waist:

Rows 16–20: SS for 5 rows.

Row 21: *K1, inc 1 st*, rep from * to * to end of row, ending with a K1 [46 sts].

To shape the chest:

Rows 22–28: SS for 7 rows.

To shape the breasts:

Row 29: K15, inc in each of next 16 sts, K15 [62 sts].

Rows 30–34: SS for 5 rows.

To shape the shoulders:

Row 35: K13, inc in next 2 sts, K2tog sixteen times, inc in next 2 sts, K13 [50 sts].

Rows 36–38: SS for 3 rows.

Row 39: K13, K2tog twice, K16, K2tog twice, K13 [46 sts].

Row 40: purl.

Row 41: K2tog along row [23 sts].

Row 42: purl.

Row 43: *K2tog, K1*, rep from * to * to last 2 sts, K2tog [15 sts].

Row 44: P2tog at each end of row [13 sts].

To shape the neck:

Rows 45–64: SS for 20 rows, casting off on last row.

Arms

Make two.

Using 8-ply (DK) yarn in off-white and 3mm (UK 11, US 3) needles, cast on 3 sts.

Row 1: inc in each st [6 sts].

Row 2: purl.

Row 3: inc 1 st at each end of row [8 sts].

Row 4: purl.

Row 5: inc 1 st at each end of row [10 sts].

Row 6: purl.

Row 7: inc 1 st at each end of row [12 sts].

Row 8: purl.

Row 9: inc 1 st at each end of row [14 sts].

Row 10: purl.

Row 11: inc 1 st at each end of row [16 sts].

Rows 12–15: SS for 4 rows.

Row 16: cast on 5 sts, purl to end of row [21 sts].

Row 17: cast on 5 sts, knit to end of row [26 sts].

Row 18: purl.

Row 19: cast off 5 sts, knit to end of row [21 sts].

Row 20: cast off 5 sts, purl to end of row [16 sts].

Row 21: K2tog at each end of row [14 sts].

Row 22: P2tog at each end of row [12 sts].

Rows 23–58: SS for 36 rows.

Row 59: K2tog at each end of row [10 sts].

Row 60: purl.

Row 61: K2tog at each end of row [8 sts].

Row 62: purl.

Row 63: K2tog at each end of row [6 sts].

Row 64: purl.

Row 65: K2tog three times [3 sts].

Row 66: cast off purlwise.

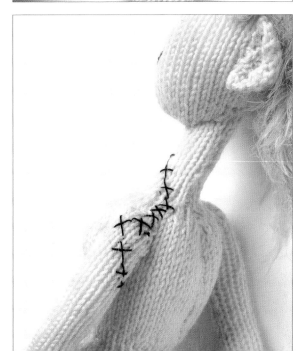

Legs

Make two.

Use 8-ply (DK) yarn in black for one leg, and black and red for the other leg. Start the striped leg with black yarn, change to red at row 5 then continue alternating two rows of red and two rows of black along the entire leg.

Using 3mm (UK 11, US 3) needles, cast on 3 sts.

Starting at the toe:

Row 1: inc in each st [6 sts].
Row 2: purl.
Row 3: inc in each st [12 sts].
Row 4: purl.
Row 5: inc 1 st at each end of row [14 sts].
Row 6: purl.
Row 7: inc 1 st at each end of row [16 sts].
Row 8: purl.
Row 9: inc 1 st at each end of row [18 sts].
Row 10: purl.
Row 11: inc 1 st at each end of row [20 sts].
Rows 12–18: SS for 7 rows.

To shape the heel:

Row 19: cast on 7 sts, knit to end of row [27 sts].
Row 20: cast on 7 sts, purl to end of row [34 sts].
Row 21: K2tog at each end of row [32 sts].
Row 22: purl.
Row 23: K2tog at each end of row [30 sts].
Row 24: P2tog at each end of row [28 sts].
Row 25: K2tog five times, K8, K2tog five times [18 sts].
Row 26: P2tog three times, P6, P2tog three times [12 sts].

To start the leg:

Rows 27–32: SS for 6 rows.

To shape the calf:

Row 33: inc 1 st at each end of row [14 sts].
Rows 34–38: SS for 5 rows.
Row 39: inc 1 st at each end of row [16 sts].
Rows 40–42: SS for 3 rows.
Row 43: inc 1 st at each end of row [18 sts].
Rows 44–48: SS for 5 rows.
Row 49: inc 1 st at each end of row [20 sts].
Rows 50–104: SS for 55 rows, casting off on last row.

Scar

Sew on Patience's characteristic scar using cross stitches worked using a single strand of black embroidery thread.

FACE

Eyes

Start by pinning the felt shapes for the eyes to the face, with the edge of the upper eyelid, the iris and the pupil drawn on to each one, using the photograph below right for reference. Notice how the eyes slope down strongly towards the nose and both irises are turned inwards, giving Patience her characteristic manic gaze. Remember to catch in the knitted stitches underneath as you embroider the eyes to secure them to the face, and to use two or three strands of six-stranded embroidery thread.

1. Begin by using satin stitch and purple embroidery thread to colour the irises, or colour them using a fine-tipped marker pen if you prefer.

2. Using the same thread, use satin stitch to fill in the upper eyelids (between the line you drew on and the upper edge of the felt).

3. Outline the upper eyelids in the same colour using either tiny satin stitches or back stitch.

4. Using black thread, satin stitch the pupil in each eye, leaving a narrow white gap between the iris and the pupil. With the same thread, outline each eye using back stitch, taking the stitching around the lower edge of the upper eyelid.

5. Use white embroidery thread to place two little white highlights in each eye.

6. With uneven straight stitches, sew on the lower eyelashes using black thread.

7. Finish the eyes with red embroidery, using straight stitches worked just within the lower rim of each eye and partway down the knitted stitch line to look like drips of blood.

8. Mark in the eyebrows lightly with a pencil or vanishing fabric marker, then embroider them on in black using irregular stem stitches.

Colouring the face

1. To give the eyes depth and drama, shade the area above the upper eyelid in purple, taking the colour down the side of the nose. Use either a fine-tipped, water-based marker pen or very thin washes of acrylic or watercolour paint.

2. Colour the nostrils using dots of brown paint or ink.

Templates for eyes and mouth.

Mouth

1. Start by pinning the felt shape for the mouth on to the face. I have used a variegated red embroidery thread to get an interesting texture on the lips. Alternatively, choose a bright red thread and introduce other shades using marker pens later.

2. Use satin stitch to form the upper then the lower lip. Catch some of the knitted surface as you stitch to secure the mouth to the face.

3. Define the lips with a line of back stitches between the upper and lower lips and around the outside of the lips if you wish. You may also like to shape the mouth a little by pulling the embroidery thread at the outer corners of the mouth through to the back of the head and stitching it in place.

23

HAIR

Patience has wild, wispy, white and pastel-coloured hair; eyelash yarn is perfect for making this type of hair.

1. First, make the base hair for the back of the head. Wind yarn around a standard-sized paperback book and slip it off, without cutting through the loops, so you have a circle of wound yarn.

2. Place the hair on to the back of the doll's head, stitching it to the head across the top of the circle of yarn where a centre parting would be. Stitch the other side of the circle of yarn to the base of the skull. Spread out the excess yarn so that it covers the doll's head and cascades down her back. Stitch it in place here and there to secure it.

3. Repeat step 1 twice to make two more thick bundles of yarn. These will form the bunches of hair on each side of Patience's head. Remove each bundle from the book by cutting through the loops along one end.

4. Wrap an elastic hairband around the cut ends of each bundle to hold them firmly in place. Lay this end of each bundle high up on the doll's head, one bundle on each side, and stitch it in place.

5. Adjust the hair, as necessary, to achieve the desired look.

CLOTHES

Dress

Make one.
Using 5-ply (sport) yarn in dark purple and 4mm (UK 8, US 6) needles, cast on 46 sts.

Rows 1–30: SS for 30 rows.

Row 31: *K1, K2tog*, rep from * to * to end of row, ending with a K1 [31 sts].

Rows 32–36: SS for 5 rows.

Row 37: *inc 1 st, K4*, rep from * to * to end of row, ending with inc 1 st [38 sts].

Rows 38–46: SS for 9 rows.

Row 47: inc 1 st, K11, inc 1 st, K12, inc 1 st, K11, inc 1 st [42 sts].

Rows 48–52: SS for 5 rows.

Row 53: knit and cast off.

Shoulder straps

Make two.
Cast on 8 sts.
Rows 1–20: SS and cast off.

To make up

1. Fold the dress in half lengthways, right sides together. Backstitch from the hem to the top. For a tight fit, squeeze Patience into her dress and sew up the seam from top to bottom. Otherwise, leave a 1–2cm (about ¾in) opening at the top of the dress and apply press studs to hold it shut. Turn over a hem of approximately 1cm (½in) and hem stitch all round. Press with a cool iron to help flatten.

2. With the dress in position on the doll, pin on the shoulder straps from the front of the dress to the back. If there is any excess strap, tuck it into the top of the dress at the back. Stitch the straps in place but make sure you do not stitch through the doll's body.

3. Attach the black fabric rose to the front of the dress.

Fingerless gloves

Make two.

Using 4-ply (fingering) yarn in black and 7mm (UK 2, US 11) needles, cast on 10 sts.

Rows 1–26: SS and cast off.

To make up

Fold each glove in half lengthways, right sides together. At one end of each glove, back stitch for no more than 1cm (½in) and tie off. Leave a gap (for the thumb) of about another 1cm (½in) and then back stitch to the end of the glove. Turn right side out.

Boots

Make two.

Using 8-ply (DK) yarn in black and 4mm (UK 8, US 6) needles, cast on 3 sts.

Row 1: inc in each st [6 sts].

Row 2: purl.

Row 3: inc in each st [12 sts].

Row 4: purl.

Row 5: inc 1 st at each end of row [14 sts].

Row 6: purl.

Row 7: inc 1 st at each end of row [16 sts].

Row 8: purl.

Row 9: inc 1 st at each end of row [18 sts].

Row 10: purl.

Row 11: inc 1 st at each end of row [20 sts].

Rows 12–18: SS for 7 rows.

Row 19: cast on 7 sts, knit to end of row [27 sts].

Row 20: cast on 7 sts, purl to end of row [34 sts].

Row 21: K2tog at each end of row [32 sts].

Row 22: purl.

Row 23: K2tog at each end of row [30 sts].

Row 24: P2tog at each end of row [28 sts].

Row 25: K2tog five times, K8, K2tog five times [18 sts].

Row 26: P2tog three times, P6, P2tog three times [12 sts].

Rows 27–32: SS for 6 rows.

Row 33: inc 1 st at each end of row [14 sts].

Rows 34–38: SS for 5 rows.

Row 39: inc 1 st at each end of row [16 sts].

Rows 40–42: SS for 3 rows.

Row 43: inc 1 st at each end of row [18 sts].

Rows 44–48: SS for 5 rows.

Row 49: inc 1 st at each end of row [20 sts].

Rows 50–64: SS and cast off.

Note: you can make the boots longer if you wish, or shorter, by stopping anywhere after row 27 and casting off.

To make up

1. Fold each boot in half lengthways with right sides together and back stitch from the toe to the top of the boot. Turn right side out and neaten any loose ends.

2. Use the same method to shape the boots as you used to shape the feet (see page 13).

Pants

Make one.

Using 5-ply (sport) yarn in light purple and 3mm (UK 11, US 3) needles, cast on 42 sts.

Rows 1–15: SS, casting off on last row.

To make up

1. Fold the rectangle in half, right sides together. Stitch the short seam.

2. Refold so that the seam is in the middle at the back. Turn right side out and stitch across the bottom to form two leg openings.

AMOROSA

This sultry Spanish Senorita isn't all she appears. Don't be deceived by her long wavy hair and stunning good looks – get closer and you will notice her deathly palour and heavy, sleepless eyes. Destined to dance for all eternity, she is the most fearsome of all flamenco dancers, with a temperament to match.

What you need

Note that these are the specific things you need in order to make Amorosa; all the general items required are listed on pages 9–10.

Needles

Knitting needles in sizes 3mm (UK 11, US 3) and 4mm (UK 8, US 6)

Yarn

8-ply (DK) yarn in off-white for the head, torso, arms and legs
8-ply (DK) yarn in black for the bodice
5-ply (sport) yarn in red for the skirt
5-ply (sport) yarn in black for the shoes
4-ply (fingering) yarn in red for the pants

Embroidery threads

Bright pink, purple, black and white

Paints

Acrylic paints, watercolour paints or fine-tipped water-based marker pens in purple and reddish brown

Embellishments and extras

Large, red fabric flower
Press stud for the top of the skirt
20cm (8in) black lace, about 1cm (½in) wide, for the bodice straps
115cm (46in) narrow satin ribbon in black for fastening the bodice and shoes
2 black rose buttons
50cm (20in) wide silk ribbon in black for the hair
Brown fake hair, for example doll's hair or a fancy-dress wig

NOTES

See the general notes on pages 12–13 for knitting and stuffing the dolls, and follow the instructions on pages 14–17 for sewing the body parts together and needlesculpting the torso and face.

BODY PARTS

Head

Make one.

Using 8-ply (DK) yarn in off-white and 3mm (UK 11, US 3) needles, cast on 3 sts.

Row 1: inc in each st [6 sts].
Row 2: purl.
Row 3: inc in each st [12 sts].
Row 4: purl.
Row 5: inc in each st [24 sts].
Row 6: purl.
Row 7: cast on 3 sts, knit to end of row [27 sts].
Row 8: cast on 3 sts, purl to end of row [30 sts].
Row 9: knit.
Row 10: purl.
Row 11: cast on 3 sts, knit to end of row [33 sts].
Row 12: cast on 3 sts, purl to end of row [36 sts].
Rows 13–28: SS for 16 rows.
Row 29: K2tog along row [18 sts].
Row 30: purl.
Row 31: K2tog along row [9 sts].
Row 32: purl and cast off as you go.

Ears

Make two.

Using 8-ply (DK) yarn in off-white and 3mm (UK 11, US 3) needles, cast on 3 sts.

Row 1: inc in each st [6 sts].
Row 2: purl.
Row 3: K2tog along row [3 sts].
Row 4: purl and cast off.

Torso

Make one.

Using 8-ply (DK) yarn in off-white and 3mm (UK 11, US 3) needles, cast on 32 sts.

Rows 1–12: SS for 12 rows.
Row 13: *K6, K2tog*, rep from * to * to end of row [28 sts].
Row 14: purl.

Row 15: *K4, K2tog*, rep from * to * to end of row, ending with a K4 [24 sts].

To shape the waist:
Rows 16–18: SS for 3 rows.

To shape chest:
Row 19: *K4, inc 1 st*, rep from * to * to end of row, ending with a K4 [28 sts].
Row 20: purl.
Row 21: *K6, inc 1 st*, rep from * to * to end of row [32 sts].
Rows 22–24: SS for 3 rows.

To shape the breasts:
Row 25: K10, inc in each of next 3 sts, K6, inc in each of next 3 sts, K10 [38 sts].
Row 26: purl.
Row 27: K10, inc in each of next 6 sts, K6, inc in each of next 6 sts, K10 [50 sts].
Rows 28–30: SS for 3 rows.
Row 31: K10, K2tog six times, K6, K2tog six times, K10 [38 sts].
Row 32: purl.
Row 33: K10, K2tog three times, K6, K2tog three times, K10 [32 sts].
Row 34: purl.

To shape the shoulders:
Row 35: K8, inc in each of next 3 sts, K10, inc in each of next 3 sts, K8 [38 sts].
Row 36: purl.
Row 37: K2tog, K6, K2tog three times, K10, K2tog three times, K6, K2tog [30 sts].
Row 38: *P2tog, P1*, rep from * to * to end of row [20 sts].
Row 39: K2tog along row [10 sts].

To shape the neck:
Rows 40–62: SS for 23 rows.
Row 63: K2tog along row [5 sts].
Row 64: purl.
Row 65: K2tog, K1, K2tog, casting off as you go.

Arms

Make two.

Using 8-ply (DK) yarn in off-white and 3mm (UK 11, US 3) needles, cast on 3 sts.

Row 1: inc in each st [6 sts].

Row 2: purl.

Row 3: inc in each st [12 sts].

Rows 4–10: SS for 7 rows.

Row 11: cast on 4 sts, knit to end of row [16 sts].

Row 12: cast on 4 sts, purl to end of row [20 sts].

Row 13: knit.

Row 14: purl.

Row 15: cast off 4 sts, knit to end of row [16 sts].

Row 16: cast off 4 sts, purl to end of row [12 sts].

Row 17: K2tog at each end of row [10 sts].

Rows 18–27: SS for 10 rows.

Row 28: inc 1 st at beg of row, purl to end [11 sts].

Row 29: inc 1 st at beg of row, knit to end [12 sts].

Rows 30–34: SS for 5 rows.

Row 35: K2tog along row [6 sts].

To shape the elbow:

Rows 36–38: SS for 3 rows.

Row 39: inc in each st along row [12 sts].

Rows 40–54: SS for 15 rows.

Row 55: K2tog along row [6 sts].

Row 56: purl.

Row 57: K2tog along row [3 sts].

Row 58: purl and cast off.

Legs

Make two.

Using 8-ply (DK) yarn in off-white and 3mm (UK 11, US 3) needles, cast on 3 sts.

Row 1: inc in each st [6 sts].

Row 2: purl.

Row 3: inc 1 st at each end of row [8 sts].

Row 4: purl.

Row 5: inc 1 st at each end of row [10 sts].

Row 6: purl.

Row 7: inc 1 st at each end of row [12 sts].

Row 8: purl.

Row 9: inc 1 st at each end of row [14 sts].

Row 10: purl.

Row 11: inc 1 st at each end of row [16 sts].

Rows 12–16: SS for 5 rows.

Row 17: K2tog twice, K8, K2tog twice [12 sts].

Row 18: purl.

Row 19: K2tog twice, K4, K2tog twice [8 sts].

Rows 20–26: SS for 7 rows.

Row 27: inc 1 st at beg of row, knit to end [9 sts].

Row 28: inc 1 st at beg of row, purl to end [10 sts].

Row 29: inc 1 st at beg of row, knit to end [11 sts].

Row 30: inc 1 st at beg of row, purl to end [12 sts].

Rows 31–100: SS for 70 rows, casting off on last row.

Templates for eyes and mouth.

Eyes

Start by pinning the felt shapes for the eyes to the face, with the edge of the upper eyelid, the iris and the pupil drawn on to each one, using the photograph on the right for reference. Remember to catch in the knitted stitches underneath as you embroider the eyes to secure them to the face, and to use two or three strands of six-stranded embroidery thread.

1. Begin by using satin stitch and black embroidery thread to colour the irises, or colour them using a fine-tipped marker pen if you prefer.

2. Using bright pink thread, use satin stitch to fill in the upper eyelids (between the line you drew on and the upper edge of the felt).

3. Outline the upper eyelids in black using either tiny satin stitches or back stitch.

4. Using black thread, satin stitch the pupil in each eye, leaving a narrow white gap between the iris and the pupil. With the same thread, work small vertical satin stitches around the lower edge of each eye, to give the effect of heavy eye make-up.

5. Use white embroidery thread to place two little white highlights in each eye.

6. With uneven straight stitches, sew on the lower eyelashes at the outer edge of each eye using black thread.

7. Mark in the eyebrows lightly with a pencil or vanishing fabric marker, then embroider them on in black using irregular stem stitches.

Colouring the face

1. To give the eyes depth and drama, shade the area above the upper eyelid in purple, taking the colour down the side of the nose. Use either a fine-tipped, water-based marker pen or very thin washes of acrylic or watercolour paint.

2. Add streaks of reddish brown underneath each eye, following the knitting lines.

3. Colour the nostrils using dots of reddish brown paint or ink.

Mouth

1. Start by pinning the felt shape for the mouth on to the face.

2. Use satin stitch and purple thread to form the upper then the lower lip. Catch some of the knitted surface as you stitch to secure the mouth to the face.

3. Define the lips with a line of back stitches between the upper and lower lips and around the outside of the lips if you wish. You may also like to shape the mouth a little by pulling the embroidery thread at the outer corners of the mouth through to the back of the head and stitching it in place.

HAIR

Amorosa's hair is made from a fake hairpiece. Attach it following the instructions on page 11. When you get to the forehead you might need to cut shorter lengths and stitch them across the hairline. To get a wild, unkempt look, pull out a few strands here and there and backcomb them towards the scalp. Finish off with a slim plait to one side, a sheer black ribbon tied around the head and a large red flower pinned to one side.

CLOTHES

Bodice

Make one.
Using 8-ply (DK) yarn in black and 4mm (UK 8, US 6) needles, cast on 25 sts.
Row 1: knit.
Row 2: purl.
Row 3: inc 1 st at each end of row [27 sts].
Row 4: purl.
Row 5: inc 1 st at each end of row [29 sts].
Rows 6–10: SS for 5 rows.

To make up

1. Wrap the bodice around the doll with row 1 at the bottom and the opening at the front. Pin the lace on to one side of the bodice at the front, take it around the back of Amorosa's neck and pin it in place on the other side of her bodice. Stitch the lace strap in place.

2. Cut a length of fine black ribbon approximately 35cm (14in) long and thread it through a tapestry needle. Attach the ribbon at the base of the bodice and lace it from side to side up the front. Tie it in a bow at the top.

3. Sew on two black rose buttons to decorate.

Skirt

Make one.

Using 5-ply (sport) yarn in red and 4mm (UK 8, US 6) needles, cast on 120 sts.

Rows 1–5: GS.

Rows 6–30: SS for 35 rows, beg with a purl row.

Row 31: K2tog along row [60 sts].

Row 32: purl.

Row 33: K2tog along row [30 sts].

Rows 34–58: SS for 25 rows.

Row 59: inc 1 st at each end of row [32 sts].

Row 60: purl.

Row 61: inc 1 st at each end of row [34 sts].

Rows 62–66: SS for 5 rows.

Row 67: inc 1 st at each end of row [36 sts].

Row 68: purl.

Row 69: inc 1 st at each end of row [38 sts].

Rows 70–78: SS for 5 rows.

Row 79: *K1, K2tog*, rep from * to * to last 2 sts, K2 [26 sts].

Row 80: P2tog at each end of row [24 sts].

Row 81: knit and cast off.

To make up

Fold the skirt in half lengthways, right sides together. Stitch from the hem to the waist, leaving a 1–2cm (about ¾in) opening at the waist. Apply a press stud to hold it shut.

Pants

Make one.

Using 4-ply (fingering) yarn in yarn and 3mm (UK 11, US 3) needles, cast on 28 sts.

Rows 1–14: SS and cast off on the last row.

To make up

1. Fold the rectangle in half, right sides together. Stitch the short seam.

2. Refold so that the seam is in the middle at the back. Turn right side out and stitch across the bottom to form two leg openings.

Shoes

Make two.

Using 5-ply (sport) yarn in black and 3mm (UK 11, US 3) needles, cast on 3 sts.

Row 1: inc in each st [6 sts].
Row 2: purl.
Row 3: inc 1 st at each end of row [8 sts].
Row 4: purl.
Row 5: inc 1 st at each end of row [10 sts].
Row 6: purl.
Row 7: inc 1 st at each end of row [12 sts].
Row 8: purl.
Row 9: inc 1 st at each end of row [14 sts].
Row 10: purl.
Row 11: inc 1 st at each end of row [16 sts].
Row 12: purl.
Row 13: inc 1 st at each end of row [18 sts].
Row 14: purl.
Row 15: inc 1 st at each end of row [20 sts].
Row 16: purl.
Row 17: inc 1 st at each end of row [22 sts].
Row 18: purl and cast off.

To make up

1. Fold each shoe in half, right sides together, and stitch up the seam from the toe to the top.

2. Slip a shoe over the tip of each foot and stitch a 20cm (8in) length of narrow satin ribbon on either side of each shoe. Wrap the ribbon around the leg and tie the ends in a bow to one side, like a ballet dancer's slipper.

JULIAN

This handsome doll is the embodiment of Gothic horror. His black, raven-like coat and boots make his skeletal face and shock of light-coloured hair even more scary. Definitely not someone you'd like to meet on a lonely road, late at night.

What you need

Note that these are the specific things you need in order to make Julian; all the general items required are listed on pages 9–10.

Needles

Knitting needles in sizes 3mm (UK 11, US 3) and 4mm (UK 8, US 6)
Crochet hook in size 3mm (UK 3/0, US 0 or D)

Yarn

8-ply (DK) yarn in off-white for the head, neck and arms
8-ply (DK) yarn in black for the torso, legs, coat and boots
8-ply (DK) yarn in red for the collar

Embroidery threads

Rust, black and white

Paints

Acrylic paints, watercolour paints or fine-tipped water-based marker pens in rust (optional), brown, pink, black and purple

Embellishments and extras

Large silver brooch for the coat fastening
Nylon hair scrunchy in pale pink and purple
3 press studs

NOTES

See the general notes on pages 12–13 for knitting and stuffing the dolls, and follow the instructions on pages 14–17 for sewing the body parts together and needlesculpting the torso and face.

BODY PARTS

Head

Make one.

Using 8-ply (DK) yarn in off-white and 3mm (UK 11, US 3) needles, cast on 3 sts.

Row 1: inc in each st [6 sts].
Row 2: purl.
Row 3: inc in each st [12 sts].
Row 4: purl.
Row 5: inc in each st [24 sts].
Row 6: purl.
Row 7: inc 1 st at each end of row [26 sts].
Row 8: purl.
Row 9: inc 1 st at each end of row [28 sts].
Row 10: purl.
Row 11: inc 1 st at each end of row [30 sts].
Row 12: purl.
Row 13: inc 1 st at each end of row [32 sts].
Row 14: purl.
Row 15: inc 1 st at each end of row [34 sts].
Row 16: purl.
Row 17: cast on 5 sts, knit to end of row [39 sts].
Row 18: cast on 5 sts, purl to end of row [44 sts].

To shape the nose:

Row 19: K21, inc in next 2 sts, K21 [46 sts].
Rows 20–22: SS for 3 rows.
Row 23: K21, K2tog twice, K21 [44 sts].
Row 24: purl.
Row 25: inc 1 st at each end of row [46 sts].
Rows 26–31: SS for 6 rows.
Row 32: P2tog at each end of row [44 sts].
Row 33: K2tog at each end of row [42 sts].
Row 34: P2tog at each end of row [40 sts].
Row 35: K2tog at each end of row [38 sts].
Row 36: purl.
Row 37: K2tog along row [19 sts].
Row 38: purl.
Row 39: K2tog four times, K3, K2tog four times [11 sts].
Row 40: P2tog at each end of row [9 sts].
Row 41: knit and cast off as you go.

Ears

Make two.

Using 8-ply (DK) yarn in off-white and 3mm (UK 11, US 3) needles, cast on 4 sts.

Row 1: inc in each st [8 sts].
Row 2: purl.
Row 3: inc in each st [16 sts].
Row 4: purl.
Row 5: K2tog at each end of row [14 sts].
Row 6: P2tog at each end of row [12 sts].
Row 7: K2tog along row [6 sts].
Row 8: cast off purlwise.

Torso

Make one.

Using 8-ply (DK) yarn in black and 3mm (UK 11, US 3) needles, cast on 44 sts.

For the lower torso:
Rows 1–24: SS for 24 rows.

For the chest:
Row 25: K4, inc 1 st, K5, inc 1 st, K5, inc 1 st, K10, inc 1 st, K5, inc 1 st, K5, inc 1 st, K4 [50 sts].
Rows 26–38: SS for 13 rows.

To shape the shoulders:
Row 39: K12, inc in each of next 3 sts, K20, inc in each of next 3 sts, K12 [56 sts].
Rows 40–42: SS for 3 rows.
Row 43: K12, K2tog three times, K20, K2tog three times, K12 [50 sts].
Row 44: purl.
Break black yarn and join in off-white.
Row 45: *K2tog, K1*, rep from * to * to end of row, ending with a K2tog [33 sts].
Row 46: purl.
Row 47: K2tog eight times, K1, K2tog eight times [17 sts].
Row 48: purl.
Row 49: K2tog at each end of row [15 sts].

To shape the neck:
Rows 50–69: SS for 20 rows, casting off on last row.

Arms

Make two.

Using 8-ply (DK) yarn in off-white and 3mm (UK 11, US 3) needles, cast on 3 sts.

Row 1: inc in each st [6 sts].
Row 2: purl.
Row 3: inc 1 st at each end of row [8 sts].
Row 4: purl.
Row 5: inc 1 st at each end of row [10 sts].
Row 6: purl.
Row 7: inc 1 st at each end of row [12 sts].
Row 8: purl.
Row 9: inc 1 st at each end of row [14 sts].
Row 10: purl.
Row 11: inc 1 st at each end of row [16 sts].
Rows 12–15: SS for 4 rows.
Row 16: cast on 5 sts, purl to end of row [21 sts].
Row 17: cast on 5 sts, knit to end of row [26 sts].
Row 18: purl.
Row 19: cast off 5 sts, knit to end of row [21 sts].
Row 20: cast off 5 sts, purl to end of row [16 sts].
Row 21: K2tog at each end of row [14 sts].
Row 22: P2tog at each end of row [12 sts].
Rows 23–58: SS for 36 rows.
Row 59: K2tog at each end of row [10 sts].
Row 60: purl.
Row 61: K2tog at each end of row [8 sts].
Row 62: purl.
Row 63: K2tog at each end of row [6 sts].
Row 64: purl.
Row 65: K2tog three times [3 sts].
Row 66: cast off purlwise.

Legs

Make two.

Using 8-ply (DK) yarn in black and 3mm (UK 11, US 3) needles, cast on 3 sts.

Row 1: inc in each st [6 sts].
Row 2: purl.
Row 3: inc in each st [12 sts].
Row 4: purl.
Row 5: inc 1 st at each end of row [14 sts].
Row 6: purl.
Row 7: inc 1 st at each end of row [16 sts].
Row 8: purl.
Row 9: inc 1 st at each end of row [18 sts].
Row 10: purl.

Row 11: inc 1 st at each end of row [20 sts].
Rows 12–18: SS for 7 rows.

To shape the heel:
Row 19: cast on 7 sts, knit to end of row [27 sts].
Row 20: cast on 7 sts, purl to end of row [34 sts].
Row 21: K2tog at each end of row [32 sts].
Row 22: purl.
Row 23: K2tog at each end of row [30 sts].
Row 24: P2tog at each end of row [28 sts].
Row 25: K2tog five times, K8, K2tog five times [18 sts].
Row 26: P2tog three times, P6, P2tog three times [12 sts].

To start the leg:
Rows 27–32: SS for 6 rows.

To shape the calf:
Row 33: inc 1 st at each end of row [14 sts].
Rows 34–38: SS for 5 rows.
Row 39: inc 1 st at each end of row [16 sts].
Rows 40–42: SS for 3 rows.
Row 43: inc 1 st at each end of row [18 sts].
Rows 44–48: SS for 5 rows.
Row 49: inc 1 st at each end of row [20 sts].
Rows 50–104: SS for 55 rows, casting off on last row.

FACE

Templates for eyes and mouth.

Eyes

Start by pinning the felt shapes for the eyes to the face, with the edge of the upper eyelid, the iris and the pupil drawn on to each one, using the photograph below for reference. Notice that Julian's pupils form the upper coloured section of his eyes, and his irises form the lower section. Remember to catch in the knitted stitches underneath as you embroider the eyes to secure them to the face, and to use two or three strands of six-stranded embroidery thread.

1. Begin by using satin stitch and rust-coloured embroidery thread to colour the irises, then use black thread to embroider the pupils. Alternatively, colour the eyes using a fine-tipped marker pen if you prefer.

2. Using black thread, fill in the upper eyelids (between the line you drew on and the upper edge of the felt) with satin stitch.

3. Outline the upper eyelid, the coloured centre and the lower edge of each eye in black using either tiny satin stitches or back stitch.

4. Using black thread, work small vertical satin stitches around the lower edge of each eye, to give the effect of heavy eye make-up.

5. Use white embroidery thread to place two little white highlights in each eye.

6. Sew a line of uneven straight stitches just under each eye using the rust-coloured thread.

7. Julian's eyebrows are rugged and well defined. Mark them in lightly with a pencil or vanishing fabric marker, then embroider them on in black using irregular stem stitches.

Colouring the face

1. To give the eyes depth and drama, shade the area above the upper eyelid in brown and a touch of purple, taking the colour down the side of the nose. Use either a fine-tipped, water-based marker pen or very thin washes of acrylic or watercolour paint.

2. Accentuate the red-rimmed look by applying pink colour around the lower part of the eye.

3. Apply black paint lightly to add depth and form to the cheekbones, the chin and around the lower part of the nose, and to enhance Julian's pallid complexion.

Mouth

1. Start by pinning the felt shape for the mouth on to the face.

2. Use satin stitch and rust-coloured thread to form the upper then the lower lip. Catch some of the knitted surface as you stitch to secure the mouth to the face.

3. Define the lips with a line of back stitches between the upper and lower lips and around the outside of the lips if you wish. You may also like to shape the mouth a little by pulling the embroidery thread at the outer corners of the mouth through to the back of the head and stitching it in place.

HAIR

Julian's short and spiky pastel hair is made from a nylon hair scrunchy. Follow the instructions on page 11 for attaching the hair to his head.

CLOTHES

Boots

Make two.

Using 8-ply (DK) yarn in black and 4mm (UK 8, US 6) needles, cast on 3 sts.

Row 1: inc in each st [6 sts].
Row 2: purl.
Row 3: inc in each st [12 sts].
Row 4: purl.
Row 5: inc 1 st at each end of row [14 sts].
Row 6: purl.
Row 7: inc 1 st at each end of row [16 sts].
Row 8: purl.
Row 9: inc 1 st at each end of row [18 sts].
Row 10: purl.
Row 11: inc 1 st at each end of row [20 sts].
Rows 12–18: SS for 7 rows.
Row 19: cast on 7 sts, knit to end [27 sts].
Row 20: cast on 7 sts, purl to end [34 sts].
Row 21: K2tog at each end of row [32 sts].
Row 22: purl.
Row 23: K2tog at each end of row [30 sts].
Row 24: P2tog at each end of row [28 sts].
Row 25: K2tog five times, K8, K2tog five times [18 sts].
Row 26: P2tog, P14, P2tog [16 sts].
Rows 27–31: SS for 6 rows.
Row 32: inc 1 st at each end of row [18 sts].
Rows 33–37: SS for 5 rows.
Row 38: inc 1 st at each end of row [20 sts].
Rows 39–43: SS for 5 rows.
Row 44: inc 1 st at each end of row [22 sts].
Rows 45–49: SS for 5 rows.
Row 50: inc 1 st at each end of row [24 sts].
Rows 51–61: SS for 11 rows.
Row 62: purl, to reverse the knit side for the cuff.
Rows 63–72: SS for 10 rows, beg with a knit row. Cast off on last row.

To make up

Fold each boot in half lengthways, right sides together, and back stitch from the toe to the top of the boot. Turn right side out and fold the cuff down. Stitch the cuff in place if desired.

Coat

Make one.

Using 8-ply (DK) yarn in black and 4mm (UK 8, US 6) needles, cast on 80 sts.

Rows 1–5: GS for 5 rows.
Rows 6–10: SS for 5 rows, beg with a purl row.
Row 11: K18, K2tog twice, K16, K2tog twice, K16, K2tog twice, K18 [74 sts].
Rows 12–16: SS for 5 rows.
Row 17: K17, K2tog twice, K14, K2tog twice, K14, K2tog twice, K17 [68 sts].
Rows 18–22: SS for 5 rows.
Row 23: K16, K2tog twice, K12, K2tog twice, K12, K2tog twice, K16 [62 sts].
Rows 24–28: SS for 5 rows.
Row 29: K15, K2tog twice, K10, K2tog twice, K10, K2tog twice, K15 [56 sts].
Rows 30–34: SS for 5 rows.

Row 35: K14, K2tog twice, K8, K2tog twice, K8, K2tog twice, K14 [50 sts].

Rows 36–40: SS for 5 rows.

Row 41: K13, K2tog twice, K6, K2tog twice, K6, K2tog, K13 [44 sts].

Rows 42–46: SS for 5 rows.

Row 47: K18, K2tog four times, K18 [40 sts].

Rows 48–52: SS for 5 rows.

Row 53: K13, turn and work on these sts only.

Rows 54–68: SS for 15 rows.

Row 69: knit to last 2 sts, K2tog [12 sts].

Row 70: P2tog, purl to end of row [11 sts].

Row 71: knit to last 2 sts, K2tog [10 sts].

Row 72: P2tog, purl to end, casting off as you go.

Rejoin yarn.

Row 73: K14, turn and work on these sts only.

Rows 74–88: SS for 15 rows.

Row 89: K2tog at each end of row [12 sts].

Row 90: P2tog at each end of row [10 sts].

Row 91: K2tog at each end of row [8 sts].

Row 92: P2tog at each end of row, casting off as you go.

Rejoin yarn.

Row 93: knit [13 sts].

Rows 94–108: SS for 15 rows.

Row 109: K2tog, knit to end of row [12 sts].

Row 110: purl to last 2 sts, P2tog [11 sts].

Row 111: K2tog, knit to end of row [10 sts].

Row 112: purl to last 2 sts, P2tog, casting off as you go.

Sleeves

Make two.

Cast on 2 sts.

Row 1: knit, inc 1 st at beg of row [3 sts].

Row 2: purl, inc 1 st at beg of row [4 sts].

Rows 3–4: rep rows 1 and 2 [6 sts].

Row 5: knit, inc 1 st at beg of row [7 sts].

Rows 6–36: SS for 31 rows.

Row 37: inc 1 st at each end of row [9 sts].

Row 38: purl.

Row 39: inc 1 st at each end of row [11 sts].

Row 40: purl.

Row 41: inc 1 st at each end of row [13 sts].

Row 42: purl.

Row 43: inc 1 st at each end of row [15 sts].

Row 44: purl.

Row 45: inc 1 st at each end of row [17 sts].

Row 46: purl.

Row 47: inc 1 st at each end of row [19 sts].

Rows 48–67: SS for 20 rows.

Row 68: P2tog at each end of row [17 sts].

Row 69: knit.

Row 70: P2tog at each end of row [15 sts].

Row 71: knit.

Row 72: P2tog at each end of row [13 sts].

Row 73: knit.

Row 74: P2tog at each end of row [11 sts].

Row 75: knit.

Row 76: P2tog at each end of row [9 sts].

Row 77: knit.

Row 78: P2tog at each end of row [7 sts].

Row 79: knit and cast off.

To make up

1. With right sides together, pin and then stitch the shoulder seams.

2. Fold the sleeves in half lengthways, with right sides together. Backstitch from the cuff to the top of the sleeve, turn right side out.

3. With the coat still inside out, place the sleeves into the armholes, pin and then stitch them in place. Turn the coat right side out.

Collar

Make one.

Using a 3mm (UK 3/0, US 0 or D) crochet hook, pick up 24 sts around the neckline and transfer them to a 4mm (UK 8, US 6) knitting needle. The first row will be worked as a purl row, with the wrong side facing.

Rows 1–5: SS for 5 rows, beg with a purl row.

Rows 6–11: change to red yarn and SS for 5 rows, casting off on last row.

Fold the red part of the collar over with the wrong sides together and stitch it in place along the neckline; the inside of the collar is red. Attach three pairs of press studs down the front of the coat, from the collar down to the waist.

SEBASTIAN

Don't be deceived by the slight stature of this good-looking fellow – he's just as dark and brooding as his taller companions – and his vampire bite is just as deadly. He will transfix you with his blood-red eyes and put you under his spell, and with his handsome coat and high boots trimmed with purple, you will be unable to resist.

What you need

Note that these are the specific things you need in order to make Sebastian; all the general items required are listed on pages 9–10.

Needles

Knitting needles in sizes 3mm (UK 11, US 3) and 4mm (UK 8, US 6)

Yarn

8-ply (DK) yarn in off-white for the head, torso, arms and legs
8-ply (DK) yarn in black for the boots
8-ply (DK) textured yarn in purple for the collar
8-ply (DK) sparkly black yarn for the cummerbund
5-ply (sport) yarn in black for the jacket and trousers
Fluffy yarn in purple for the boot cuffs

Embroidery threads

Bright red, variegated red, black and white

Paints

Acrylic paints, watercolour paints or fine-tipped water-based marker pens in red (optional) and dark grey

Embellishments and extras

4 press studs
Chunky black yarn for the hair

NOTES

See the general notes on pages 12–13 for knitting and stuffing the dolls, and follow the instructions on pages 14–17 for sewing the body parts together and needlesculpting the torso and face.

BODY PARTS

Head

Make one.

Using 8-ply (DK) yarn in off-white and 3mm (UK 11, US 3) needles, cast on 3 sts.

Row 1: inc in each st [6 sts].

Row 2: purl.

Row 3: inc in each st [12 sts].

Row 4: purl.

Row 5: inc in each st [24 sts].

Row 6: purl.

Row 7: cast on 3 sts, knit to end of row [27 sts].

Row 8: cast on 3 sts, purl to end of row [30 sts].

Row 9: knit.

Row 10: purl.

Row 11: cast on 3 sts, knit to end of row [33 sts].

Row 12: cast on 3 sts, purl to end of row [36 sts].

Rows 13–28: SS for 16 rows.

Row 29: K2tog along row [18 sts].

Row 30: purl.

Row 31: K2tog along row [9 sts].

Row 32: purl and cast off as you go.

Ears

Make two.

Using 8-ply (DK) yarn in off-white and 3mm (UK 11, US 3) needles, cast on 3 sts.

Row 1: inc in each st [6 sts].

Row 2: purl.

Row 3: inc in each st [12 sts].

Row 4: purl.

Row 5: K2tog along row [6 sts].

Row 6: purl and cast off.

Torso

Make one.

Using 8-ply (DK) yarn in off-white and 3mm (UK 11, US 3) needles, cast on 30 sts.

For the lower torso:

Rows 1–18: SS for 18 rows.

To shape the chest:

Row 19: K5, inc 1 st, K4, inc 1 st, K8, inc 1 st, K4, inc 1 st, K5 [34 sts].

Rows 20–34: SS for 15 rows.

To shape the shoulders:

Row 35: K7, inc in each of next 3 sts, K14, inc in each of next 3 sts, K7 [40 sts].

Rows 36–38: SS for 3 rows.

Row 39: K7, K2tog three times, K14, K2tog three times, K7 [34 sts].

Row 40: *P1, P2tog*, rep from * to * to end of row, ending with a P1 [23 sts].

Row 41: *K2tog, K1*, rep from * to * to end of row, ending with a K2tog [15 sts].

Rows 42–64: SS for 23 rows.

Row 65: K2tog three times, K3, K2tog three times [9 sts].

Row 66: P2tog twice, P1, P2tog twice, casting off as you go.

Legs

Make two.

Using 8-ply (DK) yarn in off-white and 3mm (UK 11, US 3) needles, cast on 3 sts.

Row 1: inc in each st [6 sts].
Row 2: purl.
Row 3: inc 1 st at each end of row [8 sts].
Row 4: purl.
Row 5: inc 1 st at each end of row [10 sts].
Row 6: purl.
Row 7: inc 1 st at each end of row [12 sts].
Row 8: purl.
Row 9: inc 1 st at each end of row [14 sts].
Row 10: purl.
Row 11: inc 1 st at each end of row [16 sts].
Rows 12–16: SS for 5 rows.
Row 17: K2tog twice, K8, K2tog twice [12 sts].
Rows 18–100: SS for 84 rows, cast off.

Arms

Make two.

Using 8-ply (DK) yarn in off-white and 3mm (UK 11, US 3) needles, cast on 3 sts.

Row 1: inc in each st [6 sts].
Row 2: purl.
Row 3: inc in each st [12 sts].
Rows 4–10: SS for 7 rows.
Row 11: cast on 4 sts, knit to end of row [16 sts].
Row 12: cast on 4 sts, purl to end of row [20 sts].
Row 13: knit.
Row 14: purl.
Row 15: cast off 4 sts, knit to end of row [16 sts].
Row 16: cast off 4 sts, purl to end of row [12 sts].
Row 17: K2tog at each end of row [10 sts].
Rows 18–27: SS for 10 rows.
Row 28: inc 1 st at beg of row, purl to end [11 sts].
Row 29: inc 1 st at beg of row, knit to end [12 sts].
Rows 30–34: SS for 5 rows.
Row 35: K2tog along row [6 sts].

To shape the elbow:
Rows 36–38: SS for 3 rows.
Row 39: inc in each st [12 sts].
Rows 40–54: SS for 15 rows.
Row 55: K2tog along row [6 sts].
Row 56: purl.
Row 57: K2tog along row [3 sts].
Row 58: purl and cast off.

FACE

Eyes

Start by pinning the felt shapes for the eyes to the face, with the edge of the upper eyelid, the iris and the pupil drawn on to each one, using the photograph below for reference. Remember to catch in the knitted stitches underneath as you embroider the eyes to secure them to the face, and to use two or three strands of six-stranded embroidery thread.

Templates for eyes and mouth.

1. Begin by using satin stitch and bright red embroidery thread to colour the irises, then use black thread to embroider the pupils. Alternatively, colour the eyes using a fine-tipped marker pen if you prefer.

2. Using black thread, fill in the narrow upper eyelids (between the line you drew on and the upper edge of the felt) with satin stitch.

3. Outline the upper eyelid, the coloured centre and the lower edge of each eye in black using either tiny satin stitches or back stitch.

4. Using black thread, work small vertical satin stitches around the lower edge of each eye, to give the effect of heavy eye make-up.

5. Use white embroidery thread to place two little white highlights in each eye.

6. Place a tiny red stitch in the inner corner of each eye.

7. Sebastian's eyebrows are rugged and well defined. Mark them in lightly with a pencil or vanishing fabric marker, then embroider them on in black using irregular stem stitches.

Colouring the face

1. To give the eyes depth and drama, shade the area around each eye and down the sides of the nose. Leave an area uncoloured just above each eye to form a highlight. Use either a fine-tipped, water-based marker pen or very thin washes of acrylic or watercolour paint.

2. Apply dark grey paint lightly to add depth and form to the cheekbones, the chin, the lower part of the nose and the nostrils, and to enhance Sebastian's pronounced bone structure and pallid complexion.

Mouth

1. Start by pinning the felt shape for the mouth on to the face.

2. Use satin stitch and a variegated red thread to form the upper lip, and bright red for the lower lip. Catch some of the knitted surface as you stitch to secure the mouth to the face.

3. Define the lips with a line of back stitches between the upper and lower lips and around the outside of the lips if you wish. You may also like to shape the mouth a little by pulling the embroidery thread at the outer corners of the mouth through to the back of the head and stitching it in place.

HAIR

Attach Sebastian's thick, black hair following the rooted method, described on page 11. Once attached, trim his hair to the required length.

CLOTHES

Jacket

Make one.
Using 5-ply (sport) yarn in black and 4mm (UK 8, US 6) needles, cast on 44 sts.

Rows 1–20: SS for 20 rows.

Row 21: K14, turn and work on these sts only.

Rows 22–36: SS for 15 rows.

Row 37: K2tog at each end of row [12 sts].

Row 38: purl.

Row 39: K2tog at each end of row [10 sts].

Row 40: purl and cast off.

Rejoin yarn for back.

Row 41: K16, turn and work on these sts only.

Rows 42–56: SS for 15 rows.

Row 57: K2tog at each end of row [14 sts].

Row 58: purl.

Row 59: knit.

Row 60: purl and cast off.

Rejoin yarn.

Row 61: knit [14 sts].

Rows 62–76: SS for 15 rows.

Row 77: K2tog at each end of row [12 sts].

Row 78: purl.

Row 79: K2tog at each end of row [10 sts].

Row 80: purl and cast off.

Sleeves

Make two.
Cast on 14 sts.

Rows 1–30: SS for 30 rows.

Row 31: inc 1 st at each end of row [16 sts].

Row 32: purl.

Row 33: inc 1 st at each end of row [18 sts].

Rows 34–46: SS for 13 rows, casting off on last row.

Collar

Make one.
Using 8-ply (DK) textured yarn in purple and 4mm (UK 8, US 6) needles, cast on 4 sts.

Rows 1–16: SS for 16 rows.

Row 17: knit to end of row, inc in last st [5 sts].

Row 18: purl.

Row 19: knit to end of row, inc in last st [6 sts].

Row 20: inc 1 st at beg of row, purl to end [7 sts].

Row 21: knit to last 2 sts, K2tog [6 sts].

Row 22: P2tog, purl to end of row [5 sts].

Row 23: knit to last 2 sts, K2tog [4 sts].

Rows 24–27: SS for 4 rows.

Row 28: cast on 5 sts, purl to end of row [9 sts].

Rows 29–30: SS for 2 rows.

Row 31: knit to end of row, inc in last st [10 sts].

Row 32: purl.

Row 33: knit to end of row, inc in last st [11 sts].

Row 34: purl.

Row 35: knit to end of row, inc in last st [12 sts].

Rows 36–60: SS for 25 rows.

Row 61: knit to last 2 sts, K2tog [11 sts].

Row 62: purl.

Row 63: knit to last 2 sts, K2tog [10 sts].

Rows 64–69: SS for 6 rows.

Row 70: cast off 5 sts, purl to end of row [5 sts].

Row 71: knit to last 2 sts, K2tog [4 sts].

Rows 72–75: SS for 4 rows.

Row 76: inc 1 st at beg of row, purl to end [5 sts].

Row 77: knit to end of row, inc in last st [6 sts].

Row 78: inc 1 st at beg of row, purl to end [7 sts].

Row 79: knit to last 2 sts, K2tog [6 sts].

Row 80: purl.

Row 81: knit to last 2 sts, K2tog [5 sts].

Row 82: purl.

Row 83: knit to last 2 sts, K2tog [4 sts].

Rows 84–99: SS for 16 rows, casting off on last row.

To make up

1. With right sides together, align the shoulder seams and back stitch them together.

2. Fold the sleeves in half lengthways with right sides together and back stitch from the cuff to the top of the sleeve. Turn right side out. Insert the sleeves into the armholes and pin then stitch them in place.

3. Position the collar evenly around the neck and down either side of the jacket, with the lapels turned outwards. Pin and stitch it in place. It may be necessary to hold the lapels in place with a stitch or two.

4. Attach a press stud to secure the jacket at the waist. Attach each side of the press stud to the inside of the jacket, so that one side doesn't need to be folded over the other.

Boots

Make two.

Using 8-ply (DK) black yarn and 4mm (UK 8, US 6) needles, cast on 3 sts.

Row 1: inc in each st [6 sts].

Row 2: purl.

Row 3: inc 1 st at each end of row [8 sts].

Row 4: purl.

Row 5: inc 1 st at each end of row [10 sts].

Row 6: purl.

Row 7: inc 1 st at each end of row [12 sts].

Row 8: purl.

Row 9: inc 1 st at each end of row [14 sts].

Row 10: purl.

Row 11: inc 1 st at each end of row [16 sts].

Rows 12–16: SS for 5 rows.

Row 17: K2tog twice, K8, K2tog twice [12 sts].

Rows 18–38: SS for 21 rows.

Change to fluffy purple yarn for the cuff.

Rows 39–53: GS, casting off on last row.

To make up

Fold each boot in half lengthways, right sides together. Backstitch from the toe up to the top of the cuff. Turn right side out.

Cummerbund

Make one.

Using 8-ply (DK) sparkly yarn in black and 4mm (UK 8, US 6) needles, cast on 15 sts.

Continue in GS until piece is long enough to fit comfortably around the doll's torso. Cast off.

Attach two press studs to secure the cummerbund at the back.

Trousers

Make two.

Using 5-ply (sport) yarn in black and 3mm (UK 11, US 3) needles, cast on 16 sts.

Rows 1–20: SS for 20 rows, beg and ending with a purl row.

Row 21: inc 1 st at each end of row [18 sts].

Rows 22–26: SS for 5 rows.

Row 27: inc 1 st at each end of row [20 sts].

Rows 28–32: SS for 5 rows.

Row 33: cast on 2 sts, knit to end of row [22 sts].

Row 34: cast on 2 sts, purl to end of row [24 sts].

Rows 35–42: SS for 8 rows, casting off on last row.

To make up

1. Place the trouser pieces with right sides together and back stitch along the two short sides (these will form the back and front seams).

2. Unfold the trouser legs and place them flat. Pin then back stitch the trouser seams from the bottom of one trouser leg, across the crotch and down the other leg. Turn right side out.

3. The trousers should fit snugly over Sebastian's hips. If they are too big, either leave a 1–2cm (about ¾in) opening at the centre back seam and secure with a press stud, or run a line of gathering stitches around the top of the trousers and pull them in to fit. If the trousers are too tight then it may be that the doll has been over-stuffed. You could remove some of the stuffing, though I do find that it is easy to squeeze a knitted doll into tight clothing without them complaining too much.

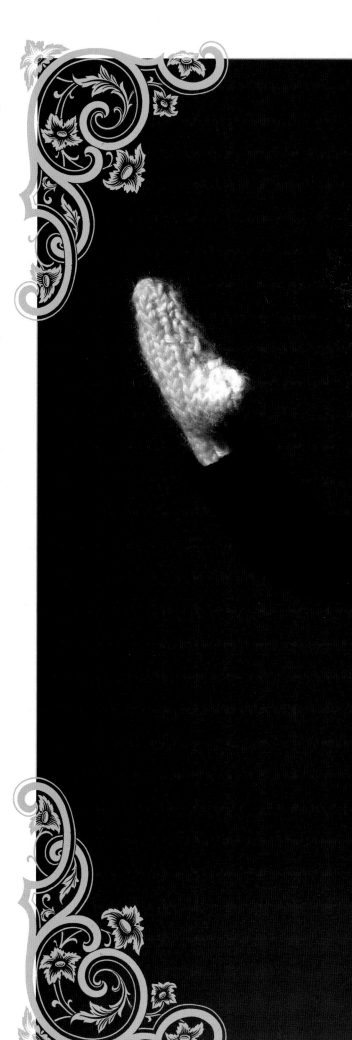

BEATRICE

This dark queen of the Caribbean guards her treasure well. Don't be deceived by her gentle smile – she's lured many a hapless pirate to his death, tempted by the promise of gold and riches beyond his wildest dreams. This is definitely a girl you'd rather not meet on the high seas.

What you need

Note that these are the specific things you need in order to make Beatrice; all the general items required are listed on pages 9–10.

Needles

Knitting needles in sizes 3mm (UK 11, US 3) and 4mm (UK 8, US 6)

Yarn

8-ply (DK) yarn in mid-brown for the head, torso, arms and legs
4-ply (fingering) yarn in black for the trousers and jacket sleeves
8-ply (DK) variegated yarn in pinks and purples for the bolero jacket
8-ply (DK) textured yarn in purple for the shoes

Embroidery threads

Orange, black, bright red, variegated red, brown and white

Paints

Acrylic paints, watercolour paints or fine-tipped water-based marker pens in purple, brown and black

Embellishments and extras

Large, red fabric rose hair embellishment
2 press studs for the jacket and trousers
4 red rose beads for decorating the shoes and jacket
8 plain red beads for decorating the jacket
30cm (12in) black lace, about 7cm (3in) wide, for the jacket
Thick black yarn for the hair

NOTES

See the general notes on pages 12–13 for knitting and stuffing the dolls, and follow the instructions on pages 14–17 for sewing the body parts together and needlesculpting the torso and face.

Body parts

Follow the instructions provided for Patience on pages 18–27, knitting every part using mid-brown yarn.

Face

Eyes

Start by pinning the felt shapes for the eyes to the face, with the edge of the upper eyelid, the iris and the pupil drawn on to each one, using the photograph on the right for reference. Remember to catch in the knitted stitches underneath as you embroider the eyes to secure them to the face, and to use two or three strands of six-stranded embroidery thread.

1. Begin by using satin stitch and brown embroidery thread to colour the irises, then use black thread to embroider the pupils. Alternatively, colour the eyes using a fine-tipped marker pen if you prefer.

2. Using orange thread, fill in the upper eyelids (between the line you drew on and the upper edge of the felt) with satin stitch.

3. Fill in the whites of the eyes using white thread and satin stitch. With the same thread, put two white highlights in the centre of each eye.

4. Outline the upper eyelid, the iris and the lower edge of each eye in black using either tiny satin stitches or back stitch.

5. Using black thread, work long straight stitches around the lower edge of each eye to form eyelashes.

6. Beatrice's fine eyebrows are steeply arched. Mark them in lightly with a pencil or vanishing fabric marker, then embroider them on in black using neat stem stitches.

Colouring the face

1. To give the eyes depth and drama, shade the area above each eye with purple, taking the colour down the sides of the nose. Leave an area uncoloured just above each eye to form a highlight. Use either a fine-tipped, water-based marker pen or very thin washes of acrylic or watercolour paint.

2. Lightly smudge black paint or ink under each eye to give Beatrice a tired, world-weary look.

3. With brown, strengthen the lower edge of the upper eyelid, taking some of the colour up into the orange embroidered area, and use the same colour to define the sides of the nose and the nostrils.

Templates for eyes and mouth.

Mouth

1. Start by pinning the felt shape for the mouth on to the face.

2. Use satin stitch and a variegated red thread to form the upper lip, and bright red for the lower lip. Catch some of the knitted surface as you stitch to secure the mouth to the face.

3. Define the lips with a line of back stitches between the upper and lower lips and around the outside of the lips if you wish. You may also like to shape Beatrice's mouth a little by pulling the embroidery thread at the outer corners of the mouth through to the back of the head and stitching it in place, then adding a touch of brown to broaden her smile.

HAIR

Attach Beatrice's thick, black hair following the rooted method, described on page 11. Once attached, trim her hair to the required length and decorate with the fabric red rose.

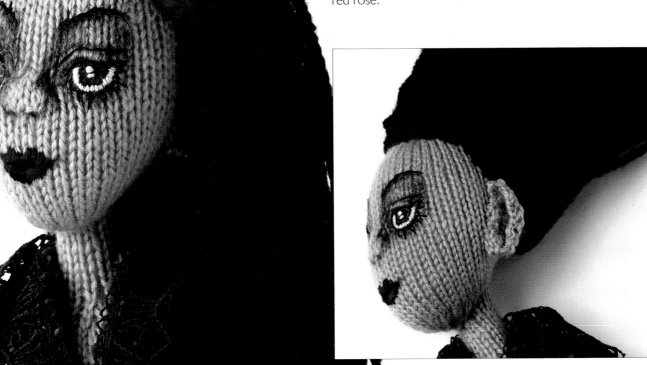

CLOTHES

Trousers

Make two.

Using 4-ply (fingering) yarn in black and 4mm (UK 8, US 6) needles, cast on 24 sts.

Rows 1–84: SS for 84 rows.

Row 85: cast off 4 sts, knit to end of row [20 sts].

Row 86: cast off 4 sts, purl to end of row [16 sts].

Rows 87–89: SS for 10 rows, casting off on last row.

To make up

1. Place the trouser pieces with right sides together and back stitch along the two short sides (these will form the back and front seams).

2. Unfold the trouser legs and place them flat. Pin then back stitch the trouser seams from the bottom of one trouser leg, across the crotch and down the other leg. Turn right side out.

3. The trousers should fit snugly over Beatrice's hips. If they are too big, either leave a 1–2cm (about ¾in) opening at the centre back seam and secure with a press stud, or run a line of gathering stitches around the top of the trousers and pull them in to fit. If the trousers are too tight then it may be that she has been over-stuffed. You could remove some of the stuffing, though I do find that it is easy to squeeze a knitted doll into tight clothing without them complaining too much.

Bolero jacket

Make one.

Using 8-ply (DK) variegated yarn in pinks and purples and 4mm (UK 8, US 6) needles, cast on 30 sts.

Rows 1–8: SS for 8 rows.

Row 9: K10, turn and work on these 10 sts only.

Rows 10–14: SS for 5 rows.

Row 15: K2tog, knit to end [9 sts].

Row 16: purl.

Row 17: K2tog, knit to end [8 sts].

Row 18: purl.

Row 19: K2tog, K4, K2tog [6 sts].

Row 20: purl.

Row 21: K2tog, K2, K2tog [4 sts].

Row 22: purl and cast off.

Rejoin yarn.

Row 23: K10, turn and work on these 10 sts only.

Rows 24–32: SS for 9 rows.

Row 33: K2tog, K6, K2tog [8 sts].

Row 34: purl.

Row 35: K2tog, K4, K2tog [6 sts].

Row 36: purl and cast off.

Rejoin yarn.

Row 37: K10.

Rows 38–42: SS for 5 rows.

Row 43: K8, K2tog [9 sts].

Row 44: purl.

Row 45: K7, K2tog [8 sts].
Row 46: purl.
Row 47: K2tog, K4, K2tog [6 sts].
Row 48: purl.
Row 49: K2tog, K2, K2tog [4 sts].
Row 50: purl and cast off.

Sleeves

Make two.
Using 4-ply (fingering) yarn in black and 4mm (UK 8, US 6) needles, cast on 1 st. (Leave a long tail of yarn to thread beads on to.)
Rows 1–5: knit 5 rows.
Row 6: inc in st [2 sts].
Row 7: purl.
Row 8: inc in each st [4 sts].
Row 9: purl.
Row 10: inc 1 st at each end of row [6 sts].
Row 11: purl.
Rows 12–23: rep rows 10 and 11 six times until 18 sts on needle.

Row 24: knit.
Row 25: purl.
Row 26: inc 1 st at each end of row [20 sts].
Rows 27–29: SS for 3 rows.
Row 30: inc 1 st at each end of row [22 sts].
Rows 31–33: SS for 3 rows.
Row 34: inc 1 st at each end of row [24 sts].
Rows 35–37: SS for 3 rows.
Row 38: inc 1 st at each end of row [26 sts].
Rows 39–41: SS for 3 rows.
Row 42: inc 1 st at each end of row [28 sts].
Rows 43–77: SS for 35 rows.
Row 78: K2tog at each end of row [26 sts].
Row 79: P2tog at each end of row [24 sts].
Row 80: K2tog at each end of row [22 sts].
Row 81: purl.
Row 82: K2tog at each end of row [20 sts].
Row 83: purl.
Row 84: K2tog at each end of row [18 sts].
Row 85: purl.
Row 86: K2tog at each end of row [16 sts].
Row 87: purl.
Row 88: K2tog at each end of row [14 sts].
Row 89: purl.
Row 90: K2tog at each end of row [12 sts].
Row 91: purl.
Row 92: K2tog at each end of row [10 sts].
Row 93: purl and cast off.

To make up

1. With right sides together, back stitch the shoulder seams together.

2. Fold the sleeves in half lengthwise, right sides together, and back stitch the seam from the cuff to the underarm. Turn the sleeves right side out and pin them into the armholes. Stitch in place.

3. Attach a press stud to secure the jacket at the waist. Attach each side of the press stud to the inside of the jacket, so that one side doesn't need to be folded over the other.

4. Thread the yarn end at the tip of one of the sleeves through a needle (as fine a needle as you can thread), knot the end and thread on three plain red beads, a red rose bead and finally another plain red bead. Pass the needle back through the rose bead and knot the yarn to secure. Repeat for the other sleeve.

5. Pin the wide, black lace evenly around the edge of the jacket, and pin and stitch it in place.

Shoes

Make two.

Using 8-ply (DK) textured yarn in purple and 4mm (UK 8, US 6) needles, cast on 3 sts.

Row 1: inc in each st [6 sts].

Row 2: purl.

Row 3: inc in each st [12 sts].

Row 4: purl.

Row 5: inc 1 st at each end of row [14 sts].

Row 6: purl.

Row 7: inc 1 st at each end of row [16 sts].

Row 8: purl.

Row 9: inc 1 st at each end of row [18 sts].

Row 10: purl.

Row 11: inc 1 st at each end of row [20 sts].

Rows 12–18: SS for 7 rows.

Row 19: cast on 5 sts, knit to end of row [25 sts].

Row 20: cast on 5 sts, purl to end of row [30 sts].

Row 21: K2tog at each end of row [28 sts].

Row 22: P2tog at each end of row [26 sts].

Row 23: K2tog at each end of row and cast off.

To make up

Fold each shoe in half lengthways, right sides together. Backstitch along the seam from the tip to within 1cm (½in) of the top. This seam will go on the top of the foot. Fold over the top of the shoe to form a cuff and finish each shoe with a red rose bead.

VIOLETTA

Poor Violetta – a single vampire's bite and she was doomed to 'tread the boards' for all eternity. But her audience left long ago, leaving no one to applaud her as she makes her dramatic appearance on the stage.

What you need

Note that these are the specific things you need in order to make Violetta; all the general items required are listed on pages 9–10.

Needles

Knitting needles in sizes 3mm (UK 11, US 3) and 4mm (UK 8, US 6)

Yarn

8-ply (DK) yarn in off-white for the head, torso, arms and legs
8-ply (DK) yarn in black for the collar and boots
5-ply (sport) yarn in red for the dress
5-ply (sport) yarn in black with a gold fleck for the waistcoat
5-ply (sport) yarn in black for the pants

Embroidery threads

Purple, pale green, black and red

Paints

Acrylic paints, watercolour paints or fine-tipped water-based marker pens in pale green (optional), red, green and brown

Embellishments and extras

2m (80in) length of 2.5cm (½in) wide black lace for trimming dress
Press stud for dress (optional)
50cm (20in) of decorative black satin ribbon, about 1cm (½in) wide, for front of waistcoat
6cm (2¼in) length of narrow black lace for choker necklace
Purple, black and off-white yarn for the hair

NOTES

See the general notes on pages 12–13 for knitting and stuffing the dolls, and follow the instructions on pages 14–17 for sewing the body parts together and needlesculpting the torso and face.

BODY PARTS

Head

Make one.

Using 8-ply (DK) yarn in off-white and 3mm (UK 11, US 3) needles, cast on 3 sts.

Row 1: inc in each st [6 sts].
Row 2: purl.
Row 3: inc in each st [12 sts].
Row 4: purl.
Row 5: inc in each st [24 sts].
Row 6: purl.
Row 7: inc 1 st at each end of row [26 sts].
Row 8: purl.
Row 9: inc 1 st at each end of row [28 sts].
Row 10: purl.
Row 11: inc 1 st at each end of row [30 sts].
Row 12: purl.
Row 13: inc 1 st at each end of row [32 sts].
Row 14: purl.
Row 15: inc 1 st at each end of row [34 sts].
Row 16: purl.
Row 17: cast on 5 sts, knit to end of row [39 sts].
Row 18: cast on 5 sts, purl to end of row [44 sts].

To shape the nose:

Row 19: K21, inc in next 2 sts, K21 [46 sts].
Rows 20–22: SS for 3 rows.
Row 23: K21, K2tog twice, K21 [44 sts].
Row 24: purl.
Row 25: inc 1 st at each end of row [46 sts].
Rows 26–31: SS for 6 rows.
Row 32: P2tog at each end of row [44 sts].
Row 33: K2tog at each end of row [42 sts].
Row 34: P2tog at each end of row [40 sts].
Row 35: K2tog at each end of row [38 sts].
Row 36: purl.
Row 37: K2tog along row [19 sts].
Row 38: purl.
Row 39: K2tog four times, K3, K2tog four times [11 sts].
Row 40: P2tog at each end of row [9 sts].
Row 41: knit and cast off as you go.

Ears

Make two.

Using 8-ply (DK) yarn in off-white and 3mm (UK 11, US 3) needles, cast on 4 sts.

Row 1: inc in each st [8 sts].
Row 2: purl.
Row 3: inc in each st [16 sts].
Row 4: purl.
Row 5: K2tog at each end of row [14 sts].
Row 6: P2tog at each end of row [12 sts].
Row 7: K2tog along row [6 sts].
Row 8: purl and cast off as you go.

Torso

Make one.

Using 8-ply (DK) yarn in off-white and 3mm (UK 11, US 3) needles, cast on 46 sts.

Rows 1–14: SS for 14 rows.
Row 15: *K1, K2tog*, rep from * to * to end of row, ending with a K1 [31 sts].

To shape the waist:

Rows 16–20: SS for 5 rows.
Row 21: *K1, inc 1 st*, rep from * to * to end of row, ending with a K1 [46 sts].

To shape the chest:

Rows 22–28: SS for 7 rows.

To shape the breasts:

Row 29: K15, inc in each of next 16 sts, K15 [62 sts].
Rows 30–34: SS for 5 rows.

To shape the shoulders:

Row 35: K13, inc in next 2 sts, K2tog sixteen times, inc in next 2 sts, K13 [50 sts].
Rows 36–38: SS for 3 rows.
Row 39: K13, K2tog twice, K16, K2tog twice, K13 [46 sts].
Row 40: purl.
Row 41: K2tog along row [23 sts].
Row 42: purl.

Row 43: *K2tog, K1*, rep from * to * to last 2 sts, K2tog [15 sts].
Row 44: P2tog at each end of row [13 sts].

To shape the neck:
Rows 45–64: SS for 20 rows, casting off on last row.

Arms

Make two.
Using 8-ply (DK) yarn in off-white and 3mm (UK 11, US 3) needles, cast on 3 sts.
Row 1: inc in each st [6 sts].
Row 2: purl.
Row 3: inc 1 st at each end of row [8 sts].
Row 4: purl.
Row 5: inc 1 st at each end of row [10 sts].
Row 6: purl.
Row 7: inc 1 st at each end of row [12 sts].
Row 8: purl.
Row 9: inc 1 st at each end of row [14 sts].
Row 10: purl.
Row 11: inc 1 st at each end of row [16 sts].
Rows 12–15: SS for 4 rows.
Row 16: cast on 5 sts, purl to end of row [21 sts].
Row 17: cast on 5 sts, knit to end of row [26 sts].
Row 18: purl.
Row 19: cast off 5 sts, knit to end of row [21 sts].
Row 20: cast off 5 sts, purl to end of row [16 sts].
Row 21: K2tog at each end of row [14 sts].
Row 22: P2tog at each end of row [12 sts].
Rows 23–58: SS for 36 rows.
Row 59: K2tog at each end of row [10 sts].
Row 60: purl.
Row 61: K2tog at each end of row [8 sts].
Row 62: purl.
Row 63: K2tog at each end of row [6 sts].
Row 64: purl.
Row 65: K2tog three times [3 sts].
Row 66: cast off purlwise.

Legs

Make two.
Using 8-ply (DK) yarn in off-white and 3mm (UK 11, US 3) needles, cast on 3 sts.
Row 1: inc in each st [6 sts].
Row 2: purl.
Row 3: inc in each st [12 sts].
Row 4: purl.

Row 5: inc 1 st at each end of row [14 sts].
Row 6: purl.
Row 7: inc 1 st at each end of row [16 sts].
Row 8: purl.
Row 9: inc 1 st at each end of row [18 sts].
Rows 10–100: SS, casting off on last row.

Boots

Violetta's boots are made separately but then stitched on and stuffed as part of the leg, giving a skin-tight look.

Make two.

Using 8-ply (DK) yarn in black and 4mm (UK 8, US 6) needles, cast on 3 sts.

Row 1: inc in each st [6 sts].

Row 2: purl.

Row 3: inc in each st [12 sts].

Row 4: purl.

Row 5: inc 1 st at each end of row [14 sts].

Row 6: purl.

Row 7: inc 1 st at each end of row [16 sts].

Row 8: purl.

Row 9: inc 1 st at each end of row [18 sts].

Row 10: purl.

Row 11: inc 1 st at each end of row [20 sts].

Rows 12–18: SS for 7 rows.

To shape the heel:

Row 19: cast on 7 sts, knit to end of row [27 sts].

Row 20: cast on 7 sts, purl to end of row [34 sts].

Row 21: K2tog at each end of row [32 sts].

Row 22: purl.

Row 23: K2tog at each end of row [30 sts].

Row 24: P2tog at each end of row [28 sts].

Row 25: K2tog five times, K8, K2tog five times [18 sts].

Row 26: P2tog three times, P6, P2tog three times [12 sts].

To start the leg:

Rows 27–32: SS for 6 rows.

Row 33: inc 1 st at each end of row [14 sts].

Rows 34–38: SS for 5 rows.

Row 39: inc 1 st at each end of row [16 sts].

Rows 40–42: SS for 3 rows.

Row 43: inc 1 st at each end of row [18 sts].

Rows 44–48: SS for 5 rows.

Row 49: inc 1 st at each end of row [20 sts].

Rows 50–81: SS for 30 rows, casting off on last row.

To make up

Fold each boot in half lengthways with right sides together. Mattress stitch up the entire length of each boot. Turn right side out. Stuff the foot area firmly without distorting. Slip a boot on to a stuffed leg as far as it will go. Ideally the tip of the leg will fit right down into the heel of the boot (not the toe). Stitch the boot to the leg around the top of the boot and repeat for the other leg.

FACE

Eyes

Start by pinning the felt shapes for the eyes to the face, with the edge of the upper eyelid, the iris and the pupil drawn on to each one, using the photographs on these pages for reference. Remember to catch in the knitted stitches underneath as you embroider the eyes to secure them to the face, and to use two or three strands of six-stranded embroidery thread.

Templates for eyes and mouth.

1. Begin by using satin stitch and pale green embroidery thread to colour the irises, then use black thread to embroider the pupils. Alternatively, colour the eyes using a fine-tipped marker pen if you prefer.

2. Using purple thread, fill in the upper eyelids (between the line you drew on and the upper edge of the felt) with satin stitch. Extend this coloured area beyond the outer edges of the eyes to create a more dramatic effect.

3. Outline the upper eyelids in black using either tiny satin stitches or back stitch.

4. Using red thread, work small satin stitches around the lower edge of each eye to make them look bloodshot.

5. Work lines of red stitching running down from the eyes, to resemble dripping blood.

6. Mark in Violetta's fine eyebrows with a pencil or vanishing fabric marker, then embroider them on in black using neat stem stitches.

Colouring the face

1. To give the eyes a tired, haunted look, shade the area just above and just underneath each eye with brown. Use either a fine-tipped, water-based marker pen or very thin washes of acrylic or watercolour paint.

2. Touch a dab of red paint into each nostril.

3. Use green paint or ink to define the outer edge of each iris.

Mouth

1. Start by pinning the felt shape for the mouth on to the face.

2. Use satin stitch and red thread to form the upper and then the lower lip. Catch some of the knitted surface as you stitch to secure the mouth to the face.

3. Define the lips with a line of back stitches between the upper and lower lips and around the outside of the lips if you wish. You may also like to shape Violetta's mouth a little by pulling the embroidery thread at the outer corners of the mouth through to the back of the head and stitching it in place.

HAIR

Fringe

Make the fringe first as the longer yarn will cover the back edge of it.

1. Wind thick purple yarn around a piece of stiff cardboard approximately 5–8cm (2–3in) wide and 13cm (5in) long. Continue to wind until the yarn is sufficiently dense to form a thick fringe.

2. Cut through the loops of yarn along one of the long sides of the cardboard.

3. Unfold the strands of yarn carefully and lie them out flat in a line. Taking a few strands at a time, place them on the front of the head, along the hairline, and stitch across the yarn from one side of the forehead to the other, adding in more yarn as you go.

4. When the fringe is complete, fold it down over the face and trim it to the desired length.

Long hair

1. Wind lengths of thick black and off-white yarn around a large book, in roughly equal proportions. When you have a thick wad of yarn, cut through the loops along one of the short ends and lay the yarns out flat.

2. Find the middle of the yarn lengths by measuring and carefully pick up about a quarter of the strands. Lay the bundle on the top of the doll's head so that the strands fall evenly on either side, overlapping the back of the fringe slightly. Stitch along the mid-line to form the start of the centre parting.

3. Place and stitch another quarter of the yarn to the head, just behind the first bundle. Repeat until all the yarn is attached to the head. Make sure that the back of the head is covered.

4. Re-establish the centre parting and tie the hair up in two high bunches, one on each side of the doll's head. You may wish to stitch the hair underneath the bunches to the scalp to hold them in place securely.

CLOTHES

Dress

Make one.

Using 5-ply (sport) yarn in red and 3mm (UK 11, US 3) needles, cast on 80 sts.

Rows 1–14: SS for 14 rows.

Row 15: K2tog at each end of row [78 sts].

Row 16: purl.

Row 17: K2tog, K18, K2tog, K34, K2tog, K18, K2tog [74 sts].

Row 18: purl.

Row 19: K2tog, K18, K2tog, K30, K2tog, K18, K2tog [70 sts].

Row 20: purl.

Row 21: K2tog, K18, K2tog, K26, K2tog, K18, K2tog [66 sts].

Row 22: purl.

Row 23: K2tog, K18, K2tog, K22, K2tog, K18, K2tog [62 sts].

Row 24: purl.

Row 25: K2tog, K18, K2tog, K18, K2tog, K18, K2tog [58 sts].

Rows 26–44: SS for 19 rows.

Row 45: K2tog, K18, K2tog, K14, K2tog, K18, K2tog [54 sts].

Row 46: purl.

Row 47: K2tog, K18, K2tog, K10, K2tog, K18, K2tog [50 sts].

Rows 48–58: SS for 11 rows.

Row 59: inc 1 st, K18, inc 1 st, K10, inc 1 st, K18, inc 1 st [54 sts].

Row 60: purl.

Row 61: inc 1 st, K18, K14, inc 1 st, K18, inc 1 st [58 sts].

Rows 62–69: SS for 8 rows.

Row 70: purl and cast off.

Sleeves

Make two.

Cast on 16 sts.

Rows 1–20: SS for 20 rows.

Row 21: K2tog at each end of row [14 sts].

Row 22: purl.

Row 23: K2tog at each end of row [12 sts].

Row 24: purl.

Row 25: K2tog at each end of row [10 sts].

Row 26: purl.

Row 27: K2tog at each end of row [8 sts].

Row 28: purl.

Row 29: K2tog at each end of row [6 sts].

Row 30: purl and cast off.

To make up

1. Fold the dress in half, right sides together, and back stitch from the hem to within 1–2cm (about ¾in) of the top of the dress. Try it on the doll and if it is too snug a fit, sew a press stud on each side of the opening. Alternatively, sew the seam up to the top.

2. Fold each sleeve in half lengthwise with right sides together. Backstitch up the length of each sleeve. Turn right side out.

3. Lie the dress flat on a table with the front face up and the centre back seam face down. Line up the seam of one sleeve with the side of the dress and stitch it in place with a few stitches. The top part of the sleeve is not attached to the dress. Attach the other sleeve in the same way.

4. Run a row of gathering stitches along the centre line of a 1m (40in) length of 2.5cm (½in) wide black lace. Pull the thread to gather the lace, fold it in half and stitch it around the hem of the dress.

5. Take a 50cm (20in) length of the same lace and run gathering stitches along one edge. Pull the thread and stitch the gathered edge of the lace around the bottom of one sleeve. Trim the other sleeve in the same way.

Collar

Make one.

Using 8-ply (DK) yarn in black and 4mm (UK 8, US 6) needles, cast on 15 sts.

Row 1: inc in each st [30 sts].

Row 2: purl.

Row 3: inc 1 st at each end of row [32 sts].

Row 4: purl.

Row 5: inc 1 st at each end of row [34 sts].

Row 6: purl.

Row 7: inc 1 st at each end of row [36 sts].

Row 8: purl.

Row 9: inc 1 st at each end of row [38 sts].

Row 10: purl.

Row 11: inc 1 st at each end of row [40 sts].

Row 12: purl and cast off.

Waistcoat

Make one.

Using 5-ply (sport) yarn in black with a gold fleck and 4mm (UK 8, US 6) needles, cast on 30 sts.

2. Pin a strap to each shoulder. Adjust the length and sew them in place, with any excess strap sewn under the waistcoat at the back.

3. Using small, neat stitches, attach the waistcoat by stitching it on to the dress around the front and neckline, and around the sleeves. Leave the back of the waistcoat unattached.

4. Using a decorative black satin ribbon, about 1cm (½in) wide, stitch the ribbon backwards and forwards across the front of the waistcoat in a zigzag pattern, as if lacing a shoe.

5. Pin the collar around the top of the waistcoat. The collar is designed to stand up, with the right side facing the front. Stitch the collar in place, gathering it slightly to fit if necessary.

Necklace and tattoo

Stitch a short length of narrow lace around Violetta's neck to make a choker necklace. Using a single strand of black sewing thread, embroider a tatoo in whatever design you like just below her right shoulder.

Row 1: knit.
Row 2: purl.
Rows 3: inc 1 st at each end of row [32 sts].
Row 4: purl.
Rows 5–26: rep rows 3 and 4 [54 sts].
Row 27: K18, K2tog nine times, K18 [45 sts].
Rows 28–48: SS for 21 rows, casting off on last row.

Straps

Make two.
Cast on 5 sts.
Rows 1–15: SS for 15 rows, casting off on last row.

To make up

1. Place the red dress on the doll then put the waistcoat on over the top. Bring it up to just under the armpits; note that the sides of the waistcoat do not meet at the front. Pin the waistcoat in place.

Pants

Make one.

Using 5-ply (sport) yarn in black and 3mm (UK 11, US 3) needles, cast on 42 sts.

Rows 1–15: SS for 15 rows, casting off on last row.

To make up

Fold the rectangle in half to form a short tube. Backstich up the centre back seam and turn right side out. Lay the pants flat with the seam face down. With the black yarn, make three or four stitches at the base of the pants in the centre to form the crotch.

MERCY

Don't be fooled by this delicate damsel's name – there'll be no mercy shown by this dark maiden if you were ever unfortunate enough to cross her path. She makes her home on the cold, rocky mountain tops where she perches, raven-like, awaiting her hapless prey.

What you need

Note that these are the specific things you need in order to make Mercy; all the general items required are listed on pages 9–10.

Needles

Knitting needles in sizes 3mm (UK 11, US 3) and 4mm (UK 8, US 6)

Yarn

8-ply (DK) yarn in dark brown for the head, torso, arms and upper legs
8-ply (DK) yarn in black for the boots
5-ply (sport) yarn in purple for the cropped trousers and crop top
5-ply (sport) yarn in black for the coat
Eyelash yarn in black for the collar, boot cuffs and eyelashes

Embroidery threads

Pink, white, black and light brown

Paints

Acrylic paints, watercolour paints or fine-tipped water-based marker pens in light brown (optional), black and purple

Embellishments and extras

50cm (20in) of black lace, about 5cm (2in) wide, for the hair
Black press stud for fastening the coat
Chunky dark brown yarn for the hair

NOTES

See the general notes on pages 12–13 for knitting and stuffing the dolls, and follow the instructions on pages 14–17 for sewing the body parts together and needlesculpting the torso and face.

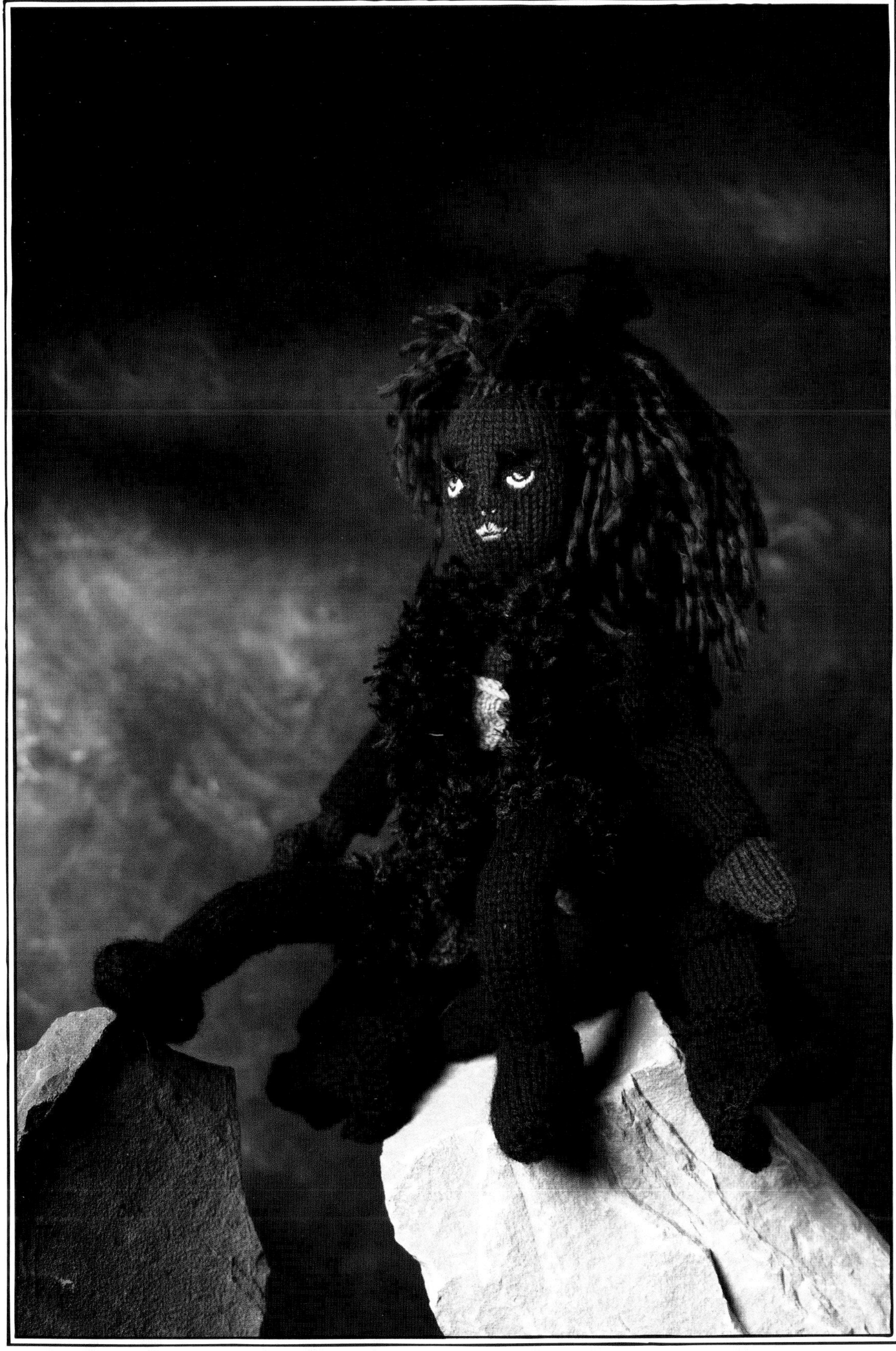

BODY PARTS

Head

Make one.

Using 8-ply (DK) yarn in dark brown and 3mm (UK 11, US 3) needles, cast on 3 sts.

Row 1: inc in each st [6 sts].

Row 2: purl.

Row 3: inc in each st [12 sts].

Row 4: purl.

Row 5: inc in each st [24 sts].

Row 6: purl.

Row 7: cast on 3 sts, knit to end of row [27 sts].

Row 8: cast on 3 sts, purl to end of row [30 sts].

Row 9: knit.

Row 10: purl.

Row 11: cast on 3 sts, knit to end of row [33 sts].

Row 12: cast on 3 sts, purl to end of row [36 sts].

Rows 13–28: SS for 16 rows.

Row 29: K2tog along row [18 sts].

Row 30: purl.

Row 31: K2tog along row [9 sts].

Row 32: purl and cast off as you go.

Ears

Make two.

Using 8-ply (DK) yarn in dark brown and 3mm (UK 11, US 3) needles, cast on 3 sts.

Row 1: inc in each st [6 sts].

Row 2: purl.

Row 3: K2tog along row [3 sts].

Row 4: purl and cast off.

Torso

Make one.

Using 8-ply (DK) yarn in dark brown and 3mm (UK 11, US 3) needles, cast on 32 sts.

Rows 1–12: SS for 12 rows.

Row 13: *K6, K2tog*, rep from * to * to end of row [28 sts].

Row 14: purl.

Row 15: *K4, K2tog*, rep from * to * to end of row, ending with a K4 [24 sts].

To shape the waist:

Rows 16–18: SS for 3 rows.

To shape the chest:

Row 19: *K4, inc 1 st*, rep from * to * to end of row, ending with a K4 [28 sts].

Row 20: purl.

Row 21: *K6, inc 1 st*, rep from * to * to end of row [32 sts].

Rows 22–24: SS for 3 rows.

To shape the breasts:

Row 25: K10, inc in each of next 3 sts, K6, inc in each of next 3 sts, K10 [38 sts].

Row 26: purl.

Row 27: K10, inc in each of next 6 sts, K6, inc in each of next 6 sts, K10 [50 sts].

Rows 28–30: SS for 3 rows.

Row 31: K10, K2tog six times, K6, K2tog six times, K10 [38 sts].

Row 32: purl.

Row 33: K10, K2tog three times, K6, K2tog three times, K10 [32 sts].

Row 34: purl.

To shape the shoulders:

Row 35: K8, inc in each of next 3 sts, K10, inc in each of next 3 sts, K8 [38 sts].

Row 36: purl.

Row 37: K2tog, K6, K2tog three times, K10, K2tog three times, K6, K2tog [30 sts].

Row 38: *P2tog, P1*, rep from * to * to end of row [20 sts].

Row 39: K2tog along row [10 sts].

To shape the neck:

Rows 40–62: SS for 23 rows.

Row 63: K2tog along row [5 sts].

Row 64: purl.

Row 65: K2tog, K1, K2tog, casting off as you go.

Feet

Make two.

Using 8-ply (DK) yarn in black and 3mm (UK 11, US 3) needles, cast on 3 sts.

Row 1: inc in each st [6 sts].

Row 2: purl.

Soles

Make two.

Using 8-ply (DK) yarn in black and 3mm (UK 11, US 3) needles, cast on 3 sts.

Row 1: inc in each st [6 sts].
Row 2: purl.
Row 3: inc 1 st at each end of row [8 sts].
Rows 4–8: SS for 5 rows.
Row 9: K2tog at each end of row [6 sts].
Row 10: purl.
Row 11: K2tog at each end of row [4 sts].
Rows 12–14: SS for 3 rows.
Row 15: inc in each st [8 sts].
Row 16: purl.
Row 17: inc 1 st at each end of row [10 sts].
Rows 18–20: SS for 3 rows.
Row 21: K2tog at each end of row [8 sts].
Row 22: purl.
Row 23: K2tog at each end of row [6 sts].
Row 24: purl.
Row 25: K2tog at each end of row [4 sts].
Row 26: purl.
Row 27: K2tog twice and cast off.

Legs

The boots are knitted as the lower part of the leg.

Make two.

Using 8-ply (DK) yarn in black and 3mm (UK 11, US 3) needles, cast on 18 sts.

Rows 1–38: SS for 38 rows.
Rows 39–46: change to eyelash yarn and GS for 8 rows.
Row 47: change to dark brown yarn and knit to end.
Row 48: *K2tog, K1*, rep from * to * to end of row [12 sts].
Rows 49–66: SS for 18 rows, casting off on last row.

To make up

1. Follow the instructions on page 13 for making up the legs, but do not stuff them.

2. Fold each foot in half, right sides together, and back stitch up the heel seam leaving the base of the foot open. Pin and then back stitch a sole into the bottom opening of each foot, easing it in where necessary. Turn each foot right side out and stuff loosely.

3. Pin a foot to the bottom of each leg and mattress stitch around the ankles. Stuff the legs firmly, but do not overstuff.

Row 3: inc in each st [12 sts].
Row 4: purl.
Row 5: inc 1 st at each end of row [14 sts].
Row 6: purl.
Row 7: inc 1 st at each end of row [16 sts].
Rows 8–16: SS for 9 rows.
Row 17: K5, cast off 6 sts, K5 [10 sts].
Rows 18–26: working on 5 sts only, SS for 9 rows. Cast off on last row.
Rows 27–35: rejoin yarn and, working on 5 sts only, SS for 9 rows. Cast off on last row.

FACE

Eyes

Start by pinning the felt shapes for the eyes to the face, with the edge of the upper eyelid, the iris and the pupil drawn on to each one, using the photograph on the left for reference. Remember to catch in the knitted stitches underneath as you embroider the eyes to secure them to the face, and to use two or three strands of six-stranded embroidery thread.

1. Begin by using satin stitch and light brown embroidery thread to colour the irises, then use black thread to embroider the pupils. Alternatively, colour the eyes using a fine-tipped marker pen if you prefer.

2. Using white thread, fill in the whites of the eyes with satin stitch.

3. Outline the eyes in black using either tiny satin stitches or back stitch. Outline the coloured sections (the pupil and iris of each eye) in the same way.

4. Work some short straight stitches in light brown over the top of the white, just within the lower edge of each eye.

5. Place a tiny pink stitch in each nostril.

Colouring the face

1. Colour the area just above each eye with purple. Use either a fine-tipped, water-based marker pen or very thin washes of acrylic or watercolour paint.

2. Brush black paint or ink under each eye, taking it from the corner downwards.

3. At this point, attach the eyelashes. Cut two pieces of eyelash yarn about 1cm (½in) long. Taper each fringe of lashes so that the inner lashes are shorter than the outer ones. Very carefully glue the eyelashes in place.

Arms

Make two.
Using 8-ply (DK) yarn in dark brown and 3mm (UK 11, US 3) needles, cast on 3 sts.
Row 1: inc in each st [6 sts].
Row 2: purl.
Row 3: inc in each st [12 sts].
Rows 4–10: SS for 7 rows.
Row 11: cast on 4 sts, knit to end of row [16 sts].
Row 12: cast on 4 sts, purl to end of row [20 sts].
Row 13: knit.
Row 14: purl.
Row 15: cast off 4 sts, knit to end of row [16 sts].
Row 16: cast off 4 sts, purl to end of row [12 sts].
Row 17: K2tog at each end of row [10 sts].
Rows 18–27: SS for 10 rows.
Row 28: inc 1 st at beg of row, purl to end [11 sts].
Row 29: inc 1 st at beg of row, knit to end [12 sts].
Rows 30–34: SS for 5 rows.
Row 35: K2tog along row [6 sts].

To shape the elbow:
Rows 36–38: SS for 3 rows.
Row 39: inc in each st along row [12 sts].
Rows 40–54: SS for 15 rows.
Row 55: K2tog along row [6 sts].
Row 56: purl.
Row 57: K2tog along row [3 sts].
Row 58: purl and cast off.

Mouth

1. Start by pinning the felt shape for the mouth on to the face.

2. Use satin stitch and pink thread to form the upper and then the lower lip. Catch some of the knitted surface as you stitch to secure the mouth to the face.

3. Define the lips with a line of back stitches worked in black thread between the upper and lower lips and around the outside of the lips if you wish. You may also like to shape the mouth a little by pulling the embroidery thread at the outer corners of the mouth through to the back of the head and stitching it in place.

4. Place a tiny pink stitch within each nostril.

Templates for eyes and mouth.

HAIR

Attach the hair using the rooting method, described on page 11. To style Mercy's hair, pile it loosely on top of her head, secure it with a hairband and tie on the lace in a bow.

CLOTHES

Coat

Make one.

Using 5-ply (sport) yarn in black and 4mm (UK 8, US 6) needles, cast on 130 sts.

Rows 1–5: GS.

Rows 6–16: SS for 11 rows, beg and ending with a purl row.

Rows 17–21: GS for 5 rows.

Rows 22–31: SS for 10 rows, beg with a purl row and ending with a knit row.

Rows 32–37: GS for 6 rows.

Rows 38–46: SS for 9 rows, beg and ending with a purl row.

Rows 47–51: GS for 5 rows.

Rows 52–60: SS for 9 rows, beg and ending with a purl row.

Row 61: K2tog along row [65 sts].

Row 62: purl.

Row 63: K2tog to last st, K1 [33 sts].

Row 64: purl to last 2 sts, P2tog [32 sts].

Row 65: K10, K2tog six times, K10 [26 sts].

Rows 66–74: SS for 9 rows.

Row 75: K8, turn and work on these sts only.

Rows 76–90: SS for 15 rows, casting off on last row. Rejoin yarn for back.

Row 91: K10, turn and work on these sts only.

Rows 92–106: SS for 15 rows, casting off on last row. Rejoin yarn for last 8 sts.

Rows 107: knit.

Rows 108–122: SS for 15 rows, casting off on last row.

Sleeves

Make two.

Cast on 25 sts.

Row 1: inc in each st [50 sts].

Rows 2–16: SS for 15 rows, beg with a purl row.

Row 17: K2tog along row [25 sts].

Row 18: purl.

Row 19: K2tog at each end of row [23 sts].

Row 20: purl.

Row 21: K2tog at each end of row [21 sts].

Row 22: purl.

Row 23: K2tog at each end of row [19 sts].

Rows 24–44: SS for 15 rows, casting off on last row.

Collar

Make one.

Using eyelash yarn in black and 4mm (UK 8, US 6) needles, cast on 10 sts.

Work in GS until the piece is about 40cm (16in) long. Cast off.

To make up

1. Fold the coat, right sides together, with the shoulder seams aligned. Backstitch the shoulder seams.

2. Fold the sleeves lengthwise, with right sides together, and back stitch along the length of each sleeve. Turn right side out.

3. Insert the sleeves into the armholes of the coat, with the inside of the coat face up, and stitch the sleeves in place.

4. Pin the fake fur collar in place around the neckline and down each side of the coat. Mattress stitch the collar to the coat. Turn the collar down and hold it in place against the coat with a couple of stitches if necessary.

5. Attach a black press stud near the end of the collar to fasten the coat.

Coat: front view (left) and back view (above).

Cropped trousers

Make two.

Using 5-ply (sport) yarn in purple and 3mm (UK 11, US 3) needles, cast on 16 sts.

Rows 1–5: GS.

Rows 6–20: SS for 15 rows, beg and ending with a purl row.

Row 21: inc 1 st at each end of row [18 sts].

Rows 22–26: SS for 5 rows.

Row 27: inc 1 st at each end of row [20 sts].

Rows 28–32: SS for 5 rows.

Row 33: cast on 2 sts, knit to end [22 sts].

Row 34: cast on 2 sts, purl to end [24 sts].

Rows 35–42: SS for 8 rows, casting off on last row.

To make up

1. Place the trouser pieces right sides together and back stitch the two short sides (these will form the back and front seams). Refold and place the trousers flat, with the seams at the back and the front. Pin and then back stitch from the bottom of one trouser leg, across the crotch and down the other leg. Turn right side out.

2. The trousers should fit snugly over Mercy's hips. If they are too big, either form a 1–2cm (about ¾in) opening at the centre back seam and take up the slack with a press stud, or run a line of gathering stitches around the top of the trousers and pull them in to fit. If the trousers are too tight, it may be that the doll has been over-stuffed. You could remove some of the stuffing, but knitted dolls can generally be squeezed into tight clothing without them complaining too much.

Crop top

Make one.

Using 5-ply (sport) yarn in purple and 3mm (UK 11, US 3) needles, cast on 40 sts.

Rows 1–16: SS for 16 rows, casting off on last row.

To make up

1. Fold the rectangle in half to form a short tube. Backstitch up the centre back seam and turn right side out. Refold the tube with the seam in the centre back.

2. Take a piece of yarn and thread it through a tapestry needle. Make two parallel lines of running stitch down the centre front and pull firmly to shape the bust. Tie off and neaten any loose ends.

3. The crop top should pull on over the doll's torso. It will be a tight fit.

GWENDOLYN

This terrifying temptress is a real party animal. Dressed to impress, she sits before the mirror in her Gothic boudoir combing her lurid pink locks and makes her plans for the night ahead. Beware anyone who catches her eye across the dance floor – you need to keep a level head when this wild young creature is on the prowl.

What you need

Note that these are the specific things you need in order to make Gwendolyn; all the general items required are listed on pages 9–10.

Needles

Knitting needles in sizes 3mm (UK 11, US 3), 4mm (UK 8, US 6) and 7mm (UK 2, US 11)

Yarn

8-ply (DK) yarn in off-white for the head, torso, arms and legs
8-ply (DK) sparkly black yarn for the dress and collar
8-ply (DK) black yarn for the ankle boots
5-ply (sport) yarn in red for the stockings
4-ply (fingering) yarn in black for the dress and pants

Embroidery threads

Variegated red, white, black, yellow and purple

Paints

Acrylic paints, watercolour paints or fine-tipped water-based marker pens in yellow (optional), white (optional), black and brown

Embellishments and extras

4 press studs
Red heart-shaped button
40cm (16in) of 1cm (½in) wide black lace for edging the stockings and pants
80cm (32in) of narrow black ribbon for the suspenders
16cm (6in) of 4cm (1½in) wide decorative black lace for the armbands
4 red fabric roses
Pink and black fake hair

NOTES

See the general notes on pages 12–13 for knitting and stuffing the dolls, and follow the instructions on pages 14–17 for sewing the body parts together and needlesculpting the torso and face.

Body parts

Follow the instructions provided for Amorosa on pages 28–35.

Face

Eyes

Start by pinning the felt shapes for the eyes to the face, with the edge of the upper eyelid, the iris and the pupil drawn on to each one, using the photographs on these pages for reference. Remember to catch in the knitted stitches underneath as you embroider the eyes to secure them to the face, and to use two or three strands of six-stranded embroidery thread.

1. Begin by using satin stitch and yellow embroidery thread to colour the irises, then use black thread to embroider the pupils. Alternatively, colour the eyes using a fine-tipped marker pen if you prefer.

2. Using purple thread, fill in the upper eyelids (between the line you drew on and the upper edge of the felt) with satin stitch.

3. Outline the upper eyelids in black using either tiny satin stitches or back stitch.

4. Work tiny satin stitches in black around the irises and lower edge of each eye.

5. For the lower eyelashes, place long straight stitches, evenly spaced, around the lower edge of each eye.

6. Place two tiny white stitches in the centre of each eye for a highlight.

7. Mark in Gwendolyn's fine eyebrows with a pencil or vanishing fabric marker, then embroider them on in black using stem stitches.

Templates for eyes and mouth.

Colouring the face

1. To add drama and depth to the eyes, shade the area above the eyelids with brown, taking the colour down each side of the nose. Use either a fine-tipped, water-based marker pen or very thin washes of acrylic or watercolour paint.

2. Put a spot of colour in each nostril too.

Mouth

1. Start by pinning the felt shape for the mouth on to the face.

2. Use satin stitch and variegated red thread to form the upper and then the lower lip. Catch some of the knitted surface as you stitch to secure the mouth to the face.

3. Define the lips with a line of back stitches between the upper and lower lips and around the outside of the lips if you wish. You may also like to shape Gwendolyn's mouth a little by pulling the embroidery thread at the outer corners of the mouth through to the back of the head and stitching it in place.

HAIR

Gwendolyn has hair made from a fake hairpiece. Follow the instructions on page 11 for attaching the hair to the head. Try some hair extensions with tiny hairclips attached to use as bunches.

CLOTHES

Dress

Make one.
Using 8-ply (DK) sparkly black yarn and 7mm (UK 2, US 11) needles, cast on 30 sts.
Rows 1–14: GS.
Change to 4-ply (fingering) yarn in black and 4mm (UK 8, US 6) needles.
Row 15: knit.
Rows 16–42: SS for 27 rows, beg with a purl row, casting off on last row.

Collar

Make one.
Using 8-ply (DK) sparkly black yarn and 4mm (UK 8, US 6) needles, cast on 30 sts.
Rows 1–10: SS for 10 rows, casting off on last row.

To make up

1. Fold the dress in half lengthways with right sides together. Backstitch from bottom to top, leaving about 5cm (2in) at the top of the seam unstitched. Attach a press stud at the top of the opening. The dress should fit tightly across the bust and be open at the back.

2. Stitch one end of the collar to the centre front of the dress, at the top. Bring the collar around the neck and stitch fasten it at the front with a press stud.

3. Stitch a red heart-shaped button to the front of the dress.

Stockings

Make two.

Using 5-ply (sport) yarn in red and 7mm (UK 2, US 11) needles, cast on 3 sts.

Row 1: inc in each st [6 sts].

Row 2: purl.

Row 3: inc 1 st at each end of row [8 sts].

Row 4: SS until stocking measures about 18cm (7in).

To make up

1. Fold each stocking in half lengthways with right sides together. Back stitch along the length of each stocking and turn right side out.

2. Take two 10cm (4in) lengths of 1cm (½in) wide black lace, and use them to edge the tops of the stockings.

3. Put the stockings on the doll with the seams at the back, and attach two red fabric roses to the top of each stocking – one at the front and one at the back.

Pants

Make one.

Using 4-ply (fingering) yarn in black and 3mm (UK 11, US 3) needles, cast on 28 sts.

Rows 1–14: SS for 14 rows, casting off on last row.

To make up

Fold the rectangle in half and back stitch up the seam. Refold the pants so that the seam is at the centre back. Make a couple of stitches midway along the bottom of the rectangle to form the two leg holes.

Suspenders

1. Measure enough of the 1cm (½in) wide lace that you used on the stockings to fit comfortably around the doll's waist, with enough overlap to secure with a press stud. Stitch a press stud to the ends of the lace.

2. Cut four lengths of narrow black ribbon, each about 20cm (8in) long, and tie two to the front of the lace and two to the back. Space them out so that they hang evenly down the front and back of each leg.

3. Dress the doll in the stockings and the suspenders, and tie the free ends of the ribbons to the lace tops of the stockings, close to where you attached the fabric roses. Cut off any excess ribbon.

Lace armbands

Use decorative black lace, about 4cm (1½in) wide, to make an armband for each arm. You will need about 8cm (3in) for each arm. Wrap the lace around the arm and either stitch it in place or secure it with a press stud.

Ankle boots

Make two.

Using 8-ply (DK) yarn in black and 4mm (UK 8, US 6) needles, cast on 3 sts.

Row 1: inc in each st [6 sts].

Row 2: purl.

Row 3: inc 1 st at each end of row [8 sts].

Row 4: purl.

Row 5: inc 1 st at each end of row [10 sts].

Row 6: purl.

Row 7: inc 1 st at each end of row [12 sts].

Row 8: purl.

Row 9: inc 1 st at each end of row [14 sts].

Row 10: purl.

Row 11: inc 1 st at each end of row [16 sts].

Rows 12–16: SS for 5 rows.

Row 17: K2tog twice, K8, K2tog twice [12 sts].

Rows 18–24: SS for 7 rows.

Row 25: purl, to reverse the knit side for cuff.

Rows 26–30: SS for 5 rows, casting off on last row.

To make up

Fold each boot in half lengthways with right sides together. Backstitch along the length of each boot and turn them right side out. Put the boots on the doll and turn down the cuff.

D'ANTON

Dark and dangerous, D'Anton is every bit as evil as his more famous cousin, Count Dracula. He sleeps by day and roams the grounds of his castle by night. Don't be tempted by his manly pose and ruby-red lips – a kiss from him is the kiss of death!

What you need

Note that these are the specific things you need in order to make D'Anton; all the general items required are listed on pages 9–10.

Needles

Knitting needles in sizes 3mm (UK 11, US 3) and 4mm (UK 8, US 6)

Yarn

8-ply (DK) yarn in mid-brown for the head, torso, arms and legs
8-ply (DK) yarn in black for the boots (knitted as part of legs) and jacket
5-ply (sport) yarn in purple for the trousers
5-ply (sport) yarn in dark red for the cloak
Red eyelash yarn for the cuffs

Embroidery threads

Black, white, variegated red and light brown

Paints

Acrylic paints, watercolour paints or fine-tipped water-based marker pens in black (optional), light brown and rust

Embellishments and extras

2 press studs
70cm (28in) of white lace, about 6cm (2½in) wide, for the shirt cuffs and cravat
70cm (28in) of narrow black satin ribbon for the cloak ties
50cm (20in) wide black satin ribbon to tie back the hair
Nylon party wig (pirate-style dreadlocks) for the hair, beard and moustache

NOTES

See the general notes on pages 12–13 for knitting and stuffing the dolls, and follow the instructions on pages 14–17 for sewing the body parts together and needlesculpting the torso and face.

BODY PARTS

Follow the instructions provided for Sebastian on pages 44–53, starting with black yarn for the boots and changing to mid-brown yarn on a knit row after about row 50.

FACE

Eyes

Start by pinning the felt shapes for the eyes to the face, with the edge of the upper eyelid, the iris and the pupil drawn on to each one, using the photographs on these pages for reference. Remember to catch in the knitted stitches underneath as you embroider the eyes to secure them to the face, and to use two or three strands of six-stranded embroidery thread.

1. Begin by using satin stitch and light brown embroidery thread to colour the irises, then use black thread to embroider the pupils. Alternatively, colour the eyes using a fine-tipped marker pen if you prefer.

2. Using light brown thread, fill in the upper eyelids (between the line you drew on and the upper edge of the felt) with satin stitch.

3. Outline the upper eyelids in black using either tiny satin stitches or back stitch.

4. Work small satin stitches in black around the lower edge of each eye.

5. Place two tiny white stitches in the centre of each eye for a highlight.

6. Mark in D'Anton's eyebrows with a pencil or vanishing fabric marker, then embroider them on in black using stem stitches.

Colouring the face

1. To add drama and depth to the eyes, shade the area above the eyelids and around the eyes with rust-coloured paint or ink. Use either a fine-tipped, water-based marker pen or very thin washes of acrylic or watercolour paint.

2. Take the colour down each side of the nose and into the nostrils.

3. Put some light brown colour into the hollows of D'Anton's cheeks, to accentuate the form of his face and his sallow complexion.

Mouth

1. Start by pinning on the felt shape for the mouth on to the face.

2. Use satin stitch and variegated red thread to form the upper and then the lower lip. Catch some of the knitted surface as you stitch to secure the mouth to the face.

3. Define the lips with a line of back stitches between the upper and lower lips and around the outside of the lips if you wish. You may also like to shape D'Anton's mouth a little by pulling the embroidery thread at the outer corners of the mouth through to the back of the head and stitching it in place.

Templates for eyes and mouth.

HAIR

D'Anton's hair is made from a pirate-style dreadlock nylon party wig. Cut lengths from the wig and glue them on to the doll's head in rows, starting at the back of the head at the base and working up to the forehead. Finish by gluing two or three locks across the forehead. Tie the hair back loosely with a black ribbon.

Moustache and goatee beard

Use small amounts of hair cut from the wig to make the beard and moustache and glue it to D'Anton's face using fabric glue.

CLOTHES

Jacket

Make one.

Using 8-ply (DK) yarn in black and 4mm (UK 8, US 6) needles, cast on 7 sts.

Right-hand side of jacket

Row 1: knit.
Row 2: purl.
Row 3: knit to end of row, inc in last st [8 sts].
Row 4: purl.
Rows 5–42: rep rows 3 and 4 until 27 sts on needle.
Row 43: knit to end of row, inc in last st [28 sts].
Keep these sts on needle while you complete left-hand side of jacket.

Left-hand side of jacket

Cast on 7 sts.

Row 1: knit.
Row 2: purl.
Row 3: inc 1 st at beg of row, knit to end [8 sts].
Row 4: purl.
Rows 5–42: rep rows 3 and 4 until 27 sts on needle.
Row 43: knit to end of row, inc in last st [28 sts].

To join the two sides

Row 44: take needle with sts for right-hand side of coat and purl to end of row using needle with sts for left-hand side of coat. Continue in purl along left-hand side of coat (coat will become one piece) [56 sts].
Rows 45–54: SS for 9 rows.
Row 55: K15, K2tog thirteen times, K15 [43 sts].

Rows 56–60: SS for 5 rows.
Row 61: K15, turn and work on these sts only.
Rows 62–72: SS for 11 rows.
Row 73: K2tog at each end of row [13 sts].
Row 74: P2tog at each end of row [11 sts].
Row 75: K2tog at each end of row [9 sts].
Row 76: P2tog at each end of row [7 sts].
Row 77: knit and cast off.
Rejoin yarn for back of coat.
Row 78: K13, turn and work on these sts only.
Rows 79–91: SS for 13 rows.
Row 92: K2tog at each end of row [11 sts].
Row 93: P2tog at each end of row [9 sts].
Row 94: knit and cast off.
Rejoin yarn for other side of coat.
Row 95: knit [15 sts].
Rows 96–106: SS for 11 rows.
Row 107: K2tog at each end of row [13 sts].
Row 108: P2tog at each end of row [11 sts].
Row 109: K2tog at each end of row [9 sts].
Row 110: P2tog at each end of row [7 sts].
Row 111: knit and cast off.

5. Sew a press stud to the front opening at the waist.

6. Form two lapels at the top of the jacket front and hold them in place with a couple of stitches.

7. For the shirt cuffs, take two pieces of white lace, each 12cm (5in) long and about 6cm (2½in) wide. For each piece, run gathering stitches along one of the long edges, pull the thread to gather the lace and attach it to the end of one sleeve, underneath the cuff.

Trousers

Make two.

Using 5-ply (sport) yarn in purple and 3mm (UK 11, US 3) needles, cast on 18 sts.

Rows 1–50: SS for 50 rows.

Row 51: inc 1 st at each end of row [20 sts].

Rows 52–56: SS for 5 rows.

Row 57: inc 1 st at each end of row [22 sts].

Rows 58–75: SS for 18 rows and cast off.

To make up

These trousers are sewn so that the wrong side of the knitting is on the outside.

1. Place the two trouser pieces with wrong sides together. Pin together the two short sides at the top of the trousers and back stitch the seams.

2. Refold the trousers so that the two short seams lie in the middle at the back and the front. Pin and then back stitch from the bottom of one trouser leg, across the crotch and down the other leg. Turn right side out.

Sleeves

Make two.

Using red eyelash yarn, cast on 16 sts.

Rows 1–5: GS for 5 rows.

Join in 8-ply (DK) yarn in black.

Row 6: knit.

Rows 7–11: SS for 5 rows.

Row 12: inc 1 st at each end of row [18 sts].

Row 13: purl.

Row 14: inc 1 st at each end of row [20 sts].

Rows 15–29: SS for 21 rows.

Row 30: K2tog at each end of row [18 sts].

Row 31: purl.

Rows 32–41: rep rows 30 and 31 until 8 sts rem. Cast off.

To make up

1. Fold the coat with right sides together and line up the shoulder seams. Backstitch across the seams.

2. Fold each sleeve in half lengthways, right sides together. For each sleeve, leave the cuff and 1cm (½in) above the cuff open, then back stitch up the sleeve to the armhole. Turn right side out.

3. Insert each sleeve into an armhole, pin and then back stitch in place. Turn the coat right side out.

4. Make a line of running stitches across the waist at the back of the coat and pull to gather.

Cloak

Make one.

Using 5-ply (sport) yarn in dark red and 4mm (UK 8, US 6) needles, cast on 80 sts.

Work in seed stitch (row 1: K1, P1 to end; row 2: P1, K1 to end; then repeat) until cloak measures about 28cm (11in) long.

For the neck:

Row 1: K2tog along row [40 sts].

Row 2: purl.

Row 3: K2tog along row [20 sts].

Rows 4–6: SS for 3 rows.

Row 7: inc in each st [40 sts].

Row 8: purl.

Row 9: (K1, inc 1 st) along row [60 sts].

To make the collar, continue in seed stitch:

Rows 10–14: inc 1 st at each end of row [70 sts].

Row 15: knit and cast off.

To make up

Sew a length of narrow black ribbon around the stocking-stitched neck of the cloak, leaving sufficiently long ends to tie together at the front.

Boot cuffs

Make two.

Finish each boot with a cuff knitted in 8-ply (DK) yarn in black and 3mm (UK 11, US 3) needles.

Cast on 14 sts.

Rows 1–10: GS for 10 rows, casting off on last row.

Fold each boot cuff around the top of a boot and stitch it on.

Cravat

Take a 40cm (16in) length of wide lace (the same lace that you used for the shirt cuffs) and gather the central 20cm (8in) section tightly. Sew a press stud to the ends of the lace to secure the cravat at the back of the doll's neck.

Index